Sabine Baring-Gould

**Post-mediaeval preachers**

Some account of the most celebrated preachers of the 15th, 16th, & 17th centuries

Sabine Baring-Gould

**Post-mediaeval preachers**
*Some account of the most celebrated preachers of the 15th, 16th, & 17th centuries*

ISBN/EAN: 9783337264802

Printed in Europe, USA, Canada, Australia, Japan

Cover: Foto ©ninafisch / pixelio.de

More available books at **www.hansebooks.com**

# POST-MEDIÆVAL PREACHERS.

LONDON:
GILBERT AND RIVINGTON, PRINTERS,
ST. JOHN'S SQUARE.

Some account of the most celebrated Post Mediæval Preachers.
by
S. Baring Gould, M.A.

# POST-MEDIÆVAL PREACHERS:

SOME ACCOUNT OF THE

MOST CELEBRATED PREACHERS OF THE 15TH, 16TH, & 17TH

CENTURIES;

WITH OUTLINES OF THEIR SERMONS, AND

SPECIMENS OF THEIR STYLE.

BY

S. BARING-GOULD, M.A.

AUTHOR OF

"ICELAND: ITS SCENES AND SAGAS."

London,

RIVINGTONS, WATERLOO PLACE;

| HIGH STREET, | TRINITY STREET, |
| Oxford. | Cambridge. |

1865.

# PREFACE.

The following work is of Theological, Biographical, and Bibliographical interest.

It has been written with the view of bringing a class of Preachers before the public who are scarcely known even by name to the theological student, but who are certainly remarkable for their originality, depth, and spirituality.

Among the numerous Preachers of the three centuries under review, it has been difficult to decide which to select, but those chosen are believed to be the most characteristic.

The Author returns thanks to Mr. John Mozley Stark, of Fitzwilliam-street, Strand, for his assistance in the compilation of this Work, by the loan of some costly and scarce volumes not in the Author's library.

The title-page, and the Dance of Death at the head of this page, are taken from the Sermons of Santius Porta, printed and published by J. Cleyn, Lyons, 4to. 1513.

# CONTENTS.

|  | PAGE |
|---|---|
| INTRODUCTION | 1 |
| GABRIEL BIEL | 61 |
| JEAN RAULIN | 69 |
| MEFFRETH | 81 |
| MATTHIAS FABER | 100 |
| PHILIP VON HARTUNG | 116 |
| JOSEPH DE BARZIA | 134 |
| JACQUES MARCHANT | 155 |
| JOHN OSORIUS | 177 |
| MAXIMILIAN DEZA | 192 |
| FRANCIS COSTER | 206 |
| INDEX | 237 |

# INTRODUCTION.

THE history of preaching begins with the first sermon ever delivered, the first and the best, that of our blessed Lord on the mount in Galilee.

The declamations of the ancient prophets differ widely in character from the sermons of Christian orators, and in briefly tracing the history of sacred elocution, we shall put them on one side.

For the true principles of preaching are enshrined in that glorious mountain sermon. From it we learn what a Christian oration ought to be. We see that it should contain instruction in Gospel truths, illustrations from natural objects, warnings, and moral exhortations, and that considerable variety of matter may be introduced, so long as the essential unity of the piece be not interfered with.

In this consists the difference between Christ's model sermon, and the exhortations of those who went before Him.

Jonah preached to the Ninevites, " Yet forty days, and

Nineveh shall be overthrown," and that was his only subject.

John Baptist preached in the wilderness, and on one point only, " Prepare ye the way of the Lord."

They confined themselves to a single topic, and that purely subjective, whereas a Christian sermon is to be both objective and subjective. It should be like Jacob's ladder, reaching from God's throne to man's earth, with its subject-matter constantly ascending and descending, leading men up to God, and showing God by His Incarnation descending to man.

A Spanish bishop of the seventeenth century thus speaks of the Sermon on the Mount, the model for all sermons, and the pattern upon which many ancient preachers framed their discourses.

He quotes St. John, " I saw in the right hand of Him that sat on the throne a book written within and without, sealed with seven seals;" and this book, he says, is the life of our blessed Lord, written with the characters of all virtues—within, in His most holy soul; without, in His sacred body. It is sealed with seven seals. St. John continues, " I saw a strong angel proclaiming with a loud voice, Who is worthy to open the book, and to loose the seals thereof? And no man in heaven, nor in earth, neither under the earth, was able to open the book, neither to look thereon."

Who, then, was worthy to open that book? None save Christ Himself. He opened it in the Sermon on the Mount, wherein He taught all men to follow and observe the virtues which He practised Himself.

Hearken and consider as He opens each seal:—

"Blessed are the poor in spirit:" and behold Him at the opening of this first seal, poor and of no reputation.

"Blessed are they that mourn:" and this second seal displays Him offering up prayers for us, "with strong crying and tears."

"Blessed are the meek:" and we see Him meek and lowly of heart, before the judgment-seat answering not a word.

"Blessed are they that hunger and thirst after righteousness:" this fourth seal exhibits Him whose meat it was to do the will of Him that sent Him, and who on the cross could still cry, "I thirst," in the consuming thirst for the salvation of our souls.

"Blessed are the merciful:" and "His mercy is over all His works."

"Blessed are the pure in heart:" and who was purer than the Virgin Son of the Virgin Mother?

And the seventh seal opens with: "Blessed are the peacemakers;" showing us Christ who made "peace by the blood of His cross" between Jew and Gentile, between God and man.

Every sermon preached since that mighty discourse, which opened the life of Christ to man, what has it been, but a turning over of leaf after leaf in that most mysterious book?

There is something very striking in the accidents of that first sermon, that fountain whence every rill of sacred eloquence has flowed to water the whole earth; delivered, not in the gloom of the temple, in the shadow of the ponderous roof, like the burden of the law to weigh it down, but in the open air, free and elastic like the Gospel, on a mountain-top, in the soft breeze beneath an unclouded sun; the Preacher standing among mountain flowers, meet emblems of the graces which should spring up from His word, sown broadcast over the world. We can picture the scene: the twelve around Him, bowed in wonder, like the sheaves of the brethren bending before the sheaf of Joseph; and beyond, a great multitude with eager uplifted faces, a multitude hungering and thirsting after righteousness, drawing in the gracious words which proceeded from Christ's lips; whilst far below, gently ripples and brightly twinkles the blue Galilean lake, over the waters of which that Preacher walked, and the waves of which by one word He stilled. We may say with the angel, "The waters which thou sawest are peoples, and multitudes, and nations, and tongues" (Rev. xvii. 15), and see in them a type of the world once tossing in the darkness and terror of a night of ignorance without God, but now to be calmed in the daylight of His presence, and lulled at the sound of His voice.

The following analysis of the Sermon on the Mount, taken chiefly from Dr. J. Forbes, will give some idea of its arrangement:—

### *Introduction.*

A. The character of the true members of Christ's kingdom diametrically opposed to the expectations and character of the world.

>The Beatitudes, or progressive stages of Christian life (verses 3—10).
>The reward of those who keep the beatitudes

in this world (11) and in the next (12).
B. The duty of Christ's servants towards the world (13—16).

*The Subject.*

" Christ is the end of the law for righteousness."

I.

(Ver. 17.) "Think not that I am come to destroy the law and the prophets."
    A. (Negative proposition) I am not come to destroy,
    B. (Positive proposition) but to fulfil.
Negative proposition explained (18, 19).
Positive proposition explained (20).

Christ then shows how that the law is made of none effect by the Scribes and Pharisees, and not by Himself.

II.

    A. The Teaching of Christ contrasted with that of the Scribes. Perfect form of the Second Table of the Law.
1. Law of Individual Life (VI Commandment, V Beatitude) (21—26).
2. Law of Family Life (VII Commandment, VI Beatitude) (27—32).
3. Central Law of Truth (IX Commandment) (33—37).
4. Law of National Life (VIII Commandment):

On its Negative or Passive Side (III Beatitude) (38—42).

On its Positive or Active Side (VII Beatitude) (43—48).

### III.

The Practice required by Christ of His Disciples contrasted with the Practice of the Scribes and Pharisees.

First Defect of Pharisaical Righteousness, Ostentation, or Hypocrisy. God must be regarded in all our *Acts* (chap. vi. 1).

    α. In the Duties owed to our Neighbours (2—4).

    β. In the Duties owed to God (5—15).

    γ. In the Duties owed to Ourselves (16—18).

Second Defect of Pharisaical Righteousness, Worldliness. God must be regarded in all our *Affections* (19—34).

Third Defect of Pharisaical Righteousness, Spiritual Pride. God must be regarded in all our *Judgments* (chap. vii. 1, 2).

We must acquire Discernment to judge,

    *a.* How to give (3—5).

    *b.* To whom to give (6).

    *c.* What to give (7—12).

*Conclusion.*

The conclusion sums up, in three practical exhortations, the whole sermon. Such being the spirit of the Law and the Prophets, and the strictness of the righteousness required,

I. Beware of Supineness (13, 14).
II. Beware of false Teachers (15—20).
III. Beware of empty Professions (21—27).

The other sermons given in Holy Scripture are those of St. Peter, St. Stephen, and St. Paul; in all of which arrangement is discernible.

But passing from the apostolic age to those succeeding it, we find that preaching consisted chiefly in scriptural exposition, the only order observed being that of the sacred text. Such was the nature of the sermons of St. Pantænus (A.D. 180), the Sicilian Bee, so named from the way in which he gathered honey from the flowers of prophetic and apostolic fields. He is said to have travelled preaching the Gospel as far as India, whence he brought back a Hebrew copy of St. Matthew's Gospel, left by St. Bartholomew. St. Clement of Alexandria and Origen succeeded him; adding polish and refinement to the matter. These great men, so well versed in the history of the Old and New Testaments, were also probably masters of the art of preaching, though but few of their genuine homilies are extant by which we might judge.

In Africa, St. Cyprian preached with eloquence and vigour. A few sermons and homilies of St. Athanasius remain; and fifty sermons preached by the Macarii to the monks in the Thebaid. St. Ephraem Syrus, Deacon of Edessa, was a voluminous writer, and an eloquent preacher. Sozomen observes of him, that, though he had never studied, yet he had so many beauties in his style, and so many sublime thoughts, that the traces of his eloquence are discernible through a translation.

St. Gregory Nyssen says that he had read and meditated more than any one else on the Bible; that he had written expositions upon all Holy Scripture; and that he had, besides, composed many fervid and touching exhortations. "All his discourses," says he, "are filled with weeping and compassionate expressions, which are calculated to move even the hardest hearts. For who that is proud would not become the humblest of men, on reading his sermon on Humility? Who would not be inflamed with Divine fire, by reading his treatise on Charity? Who would not wish to be pure in heart, when reading the praises he has lavished on virginity? Who would not be alarmed on hearing his discourse on the Last Judgment; wherein he has described it so vividly, that not a touch can be added by way of improvement? God gave him so profound a wisdom, that, though he had a wonderful facility of speaking, yet he could not always find words to express the crowd of ideas which flowed into his mind."

Every one knows what was the success of the homilies of St. Augustine, of the two Gregories, of St. Chrysostom, St. Basil, St. Ambrose. "There were giants in those days." We will not speak of them now, as their lives and their works are well known. Suffice it to say, that they spoke so as to suit the capacities of their hearers. Sometimes they preached without preparation, and in a homely manner; seeking rather to instruct than to please.

St. Cyprian, St. Ambrose, and St. Leo, among the Latins, pass with justice for the most eloquent orators of their time. St. Augustine is more simple than they;

but he preached in the small town of Hippo, to shopkeepers and labourers.

In the age after Augustine, perhaps the most famous preacher was Salvian (390—484), surnamed the Master of Bishops, not that he ever was a Bishop himself, but because so many of his pupils at Lerins became eventually prelates in Gaul. Among the most eminent of these was St. Cæsarius of Arles (470—542), son of the Count of Chalons. He passed his youth in the shadow of the cloister of Lerins, and left it only to succeed the first fathers of that peaceful isle, Honoratus and Hilary, upon the archiepiscopal throne of Arles. He was for half a century the most illustrious and most influential of the Bishops of Southern Gaul. He presided over four Councils, and directed the great controversies of his time. He was passionately beloved by his flock, whose hearts he swayed with his fervid eloquence, of which 130 still extant sermons bear the indelible stamp. Another of the early preachers of Gaul was St. Eucher (434), whom Bossuet calls "the Great;" and he, too, issued from that great nursery of saints, the Isle of Lerins.

Valerian of Cemele (450), has left behind him sermons plain and sound, but devoid of eloquence. Basil of Seleucia was a preacher of fame in the East. Photius says, that "his discourse is figurative and lofty. He observes, as much as any man, an even tone. He has united clearness with agreeableness, but his tropes and figures are very troublesome. By these he wearies his hearer always, and creates in him a bad opinion of himself, as an ignorant person, incapable of blending art with nature, and powerless to keep from excess."

Photius is rather too hard on Basil, whose sermons are really stirring and good. The discourses of Andrew of Crete (740) are also excellent; those of John Damascene are poor.

Turning to England, we shall find Bede instructing our Anglo-Saxon forefathers in the faith of Christ and in the mysteries of the Gospel; and Alfric, in 990, compiling homilies in the vulgar tongue, to the number of eighty, and, among others, that famous one on the doctrine of the Holy Eucharist, which Matthew Parker could flourish in the face of his Romish opponents, saying, "What now is become of your boasted argument of apostolic tradition? see here that the novelties with which you charge us are older than the doctrines which you oppose to them!"

Wulfstan, Archbishop of York (1003), is known through one remarkable sermon, "Sermo Lupi ad Anglos quando Dani maxime persecuti sunt eos."

We have now arrived at the true middle ages, and I will say but little of the history of preaching in that period, as it has already been treated of by that distinguished ecclesiastical scholar, Dr. Neale, in his volume "Mediæval Sermons." And, indeed, but for his labours, the bulk of this introduction would necessarily have been extended beyond its due limits, for the middle ages teemed with preachers, and preachers very striking for their originality and depth. The monasteries were great nurseries of preachers, sending forth continually multitudes of carefully trained and orthodox teachers. These preaching monks and friars exercised an immense influence over the uneducated laity, and for long they worked in harmony with the secular clergy. Let me give one instance from a chronicler of the thirteenth century, Jacques de Vitry, who has left us some interesting details concerning a very celebrated preacher of his time, Foulque de Neuilly. "He excited to such an extent all people, not only of the lower orders, but kings and princes as well, by his few and simple words, that none dare oppose him. People rushed in crowds from distant countries to hear him, and to see the miracles wrought by God through him. . . . Those who were able to tear and preserve the smallest fragment of his dress, esteemed themselves happy. Besides, as his clothes were in great request, and as the multitude were constantly tearing them off him, he was obliged to have a new cassock nearly every day. And as the mob commonly pressed upon him in an intolerable manner, he struck the most troublesome with a stick he held, and drove them back, or he would have been suffocated by the throng eager to touch him. And, although he sometimes wounded those whom he struck, yet they were by no means offended, and did not murmur, but, in the excess of their devotion, and the strength of their faith, kissed their own blood, as though it had been sanctified by the man of God.

"One day, as a man was engaged in ripping his cassock with considerable violence, he spoke to the crowd thus, 'Do not rend my garments, which have never been blessed: see! I will give my benediction to the clothes of this man.' Then he made the sign of the cross, and at once the people tore to rags the man's dress, so that each obtained a shred."

Pass we now to the wane of sacred eloquence at the close of the fourteenth century. By this time pulpit oratory had become sadly debased, though still a few noble orators, as Savonarola at Florence, Louis of Granada in Spain, and Philip of Narni at Rome, shone as lights.

In the place of earnestness came affectation: the natural movement of the body, when the feelings of the preacher are roused, was replaced by studied gestures; the object of the orator was rather the exhibition of his own learning than the edification of his hearers, and the lack of matter in sermons was supplied by profanity and buffoonery. Preachers became the slaves of rule, their sermons were stretched on the same Procrustean bed, and were clipped or distorted to fit the required shape. By this means all natural eloquence was stifled; every action of the body, every modulation of the voice, was according to canon; and to such an extent did this run, that some preachers made it a matter of rule to cough at fixed intervals, believing that they were thereby adding grace to their declamation. In some old MS. sermons, marginal notes to the following effect may be found: "Sit down—stand up—mop yourself—ahem! ahem!—now shriek like a devil."

Such is a sermon preached by Oliver Maillard, and printed with these marginal notes at Bruges in 1500, black letter, quarto. Balzac describes a lesson given by an aged doctor to a young bachelor on the art of preaching, and it consisted of this—"Bang the pulpit; look at the crucifix with rolling eyes; say nothing to the purpose,—and you *will* be a great preacher."

Throughout the fourteenth century sermons were for the most part hammered out on the same miserable block. The same text perhaps served for an Advent or a Lenten series. Maillard in the next century preached sixty-eight sermons on the text, " Come up . . . unto the mount " (Exod. xxxiv. 2); and he took for his text throughout Advent, Christmas, and the festivals immediately following—in all forty-four sermons—the words of St. James i. 21, " Wherefore lay apart all filthiness and superfluity of naughtiness, and receive with meekness the engrafted word, which is able to save your souls."

The preacher having given out his text, pronounced a long exordium, in no way to the purpose, containing some scriptural allegory, some supposed fact from natural history, or a story extracted from a classic historian. He then returned to his text and began to discuss two questions, one in theology, the other in civil or canon law, remotely connected with it. On the theological question he quoted the sentiments of the schoolmen, on the other he cited legal authorities.

He then proceeded to divide his subject under heads, each of which was again subdivided, and each subdivision was supported by the authority of a classic philosopher, and illustrated by an anecdote often pointless, sometimes indecent. Indeed, to such an extent were classic allusions and quotations in vogue, that the story is told of a peasant who had " sat under " his priest for long, and had heard much of Apollo in the Sunday discourses, bequeathing his old cart-horse " to M. Pollo, of whom the curé had said such fine things."

This absurd affectation continued long the bane of the pulpit. In the sixteenth century a monk preaching on the feast of St. Peter, saw no impropriety in mingling mythology with Gospel history, and in quoting the fable of Daphne to illustrate the denial of the Apostle. "The nymph of the wood," said he, "being pursued by the shepherd Apollo, fled over hill and dale, till she reached the foot of a rock up which she could not climb, and, seeing herself at the mercy of her pursuer, she began to weep,—in like manner, St. Peter seeing himself arrested by the rock of his denial, 'wept bitterly.'" And Camus, Bishop of Belley, who flourished in the beginning of the seventeenth century, could use such words as these on Christmas Day:—"We now, skimming over the sea in our boat, come to behold the Infant born into the world to conquer it. He is our Bellerophon, who, mounted on the Pegasus of His humanity, winged by union with the Deity, has overcome the world, 'confidite, ego vici mundum;' the world, a true and strange Chimera! lion as to its front by its pride, dragon behind in its avarice, goat in the midst by its pollution! He is our youthful Horatius overcoming the three Curiatii of ambition, avarice, and sensuality! He is our Hercules, who has beaten down the triple-throated Cerberus, and who has in His cradle strangled serpents. The one crushed only two, but ours has destroyed three, the vanity of the world by His subjection, the avarice of the world by His poverty, the delights of the world by His mortification."

Sometimes preachers, carried away by their feelings,

gave vent to the most violent and indecorous expressions. As, for instance, the Père Guerin preaching on the danger of reading improper literature, could not refrain from using the following language with reference to Theophilus Viaud, who had written a very immoral poem, "La Parnasse des Poètes," 1625, for which he and his book were condemned to be burned. "Cursed be the spirit which dictated such thoughts," howled the preacher. "Cursed be the hand which wrote them! Woe to the publisher who had them printed! Woe to those who have read them! Woe to those who have ever made the author's acquaintance! But blessed be Monsieur le premier Président, blessed be M. le Procureur Général, who have purged our Paris of this plague! You are the originator of the plague in this city; I would say, after the Rev. Father Garasse, that you are a scoundrel, a great calf! but no! shall I call you a calf? Veal is good when boiled, veal is good when roast, calfskin is good for binding books; but yours, miscreant! is only fit to be well grilled, and that it will be, to-morrow. You have raised the laugh at monks, and now the monks will laugh at you."

Preachers have been quite unable at times to resist the chance of saying a bon mot. Father André, being required to give out before his sermon that a collection would be made for the dower of a young lady who wished to take the veil, said—"Gentlemen, your alms are solicited in behalf of a young lady who is not rich enough to take the vow of poverty." I believe it is of the same man that the story is told, that he halted suddenly in the midst of a sermon to rebuke the congregation for indulging in conversation whilst he was speaking. One good woman took this in dudgeon, and standing up, assured the preacher that the buzz of voices came from the men's side of the church, and not from that reserved for the females. "I am delighted to hear it," replied the preacher, "the talking will then be sooner over." This reminds me of Gabriel Barlette's dictum, "Pone quatuor mulieres ab unâ parte, decem viros ab aliâ, plus garrulabunt mulieres."

Kings even have been publicly rebuked for something of the same kind. Every one knows that Mademoiselle d'Entragues, Marchioness of Verneuil, was mistress of Henry IV. One day that the Jesuit father, Gonthier, was preaching at St. Gervais, the king attended with Mademoiselle d'Entragues, and a suite of court ladies. During the sermon the marchioness whispered and made signs to the king, trying to make him laugh. The preacher, indignant at this conduct, turned to Henry and said, "Sire, never again permit yourself to come to hear the word of God surrounded by a seraglio, and thus to offer so great a scandal in a holy place." The marchioness was furious, and endeavoured to obtain the punishment of the preacher, but Henry, instead of consenting, had the good sense to show that he was not offended, by returning to hear Father Gonthier preach on the following day. He took him aside however, and said, "My father, fear nothing. I thank you for your reproof; only, for Heaven's sake, don't give it in public again."

I have said that the preachers of the fifteenth century often degenerated into the burlesque, in order to attract the attention they failed to rivet by the excellence of their matter. Unfortunately this fault was not confined to the fifteenth century, but we find it again and again appearing among inferior preachers of the next two centuries. It must be remembered that the monasteries had then fallen from their high estate through the intolerable oppression of the "in commendam," and that learning was far less cultivated than in an earlier age. The popular friar-preachers, the hedge-priests, who took with the vulgar, were much of the stamp of modern dissenting ministers, men of little education but considerable assurance; they spoke in the dialect of the people, they understood their troubles, they knew their tastes; and, at the same time, like all people who have got a smattering of knowledge, they loved to display it, and in displaying it consisted much of their grotesqueness. The following sketch of one of these discourses is given by Father Labat, in his "Voyages en Espagne et en Italie, Amst., 1731, 8 vols. in 12mo." He says that he was present on the 15th September, 1709, at a sermon preached in the open air under a clump of olives near Tivoli.

The day was the Feast of the Name of Mary. "Those who did the honours of the feast placed me, politely, right in front of the preacher. He appeared, after having kept us waiting sufficiently long, mounted the pulpit, sat down without ceremony, examined his audience in a grave and perhaps slightly contemptuous manner; and then, after a few moments' silence, he rose, took off his cap, made the sign of the cross on his brow, then on his mouth, and then on his heart, which after the old system he supposed to be on his left side; lastly, he made a fourth sign, which covered up all the others, since it extended from his head to the pit of his stomach. This operation complete, he sat down, put on his cap, and began his discourse with these words, 'I beheld a great book written within and without,' which he explained thus: Ecco il verissimo ritratto di Maria sempre Virgine; that is to say, Behold the veritable portrait of the ever Virgin Mary. This application was followed by a long digression upon all books ever known in MS. or in print. Those which compose the Holy Scriptures passed first in review; he named their authors, he fixed their date, and gave the reasons for their composition. He passed next to those of the ancient philosophers, of the Egyptians and of the Greeks; those of the Sibyls appeared next on the scene, and the praise of the Tiburtine Sibyl was neatly interwoven into the discourse. Homer's Iliad was not forgotten, any more than the Æneid; not a book escaped him; and then he declared that none were equal to the great book written within and without; a book, said he, imprinted with the characters of divine virtues, bound in Heaven, dedicated to wisdom uncreate[1], approved by the doctors of the nine angelic hierarchies, published by the twelve Apostles in the four quarters of the globe; a book occupying the first place in the celestial library, in which angels and saints study ever, which is the

---

[1] I have been obliged somewhat to modify these expressions here; the originals are too profane for reproduction.

terror of demons, the joy of heaven, the delights of saints, the recompense of the triumphant Church, the hope of the suffering, the support, the strength, the buckler of the militant. He never left this great book, the leaves of which he kept turning, so to speak, for three good quarters of an hour, and then finding that it was time to rest, he quitted us suddenly without a 'goodbye.' I mean without the blessing, and without having spoken of the Blessed Virgin in any other light than that which served him in the explanation of his text.

"I confess I never heard a sermon which pleased me better, for I was not a bit wearied during it; and, in his style, I suspect he was unequalled. The Passion of Father Imbert, Superior of our mission at Guadaloupe, his sermon on St. Jean de Dieu, that of Father Ange de Rouen, a Capuchin, on a certain indulgence, had hitherto appeared to me inimitable masterpieces; but I must award the palm to that which I have just reported, and to do the preacher justice, he surpassed the others mentioned as the empyrean sky surpasses the lunar sky in grandeur and elevation."

I must speak here of a famous preacher of the fifteenth century, to whom I cannot afford a separate notice, and who is more offensively ridiculous than the man spoken of by Labat; I mean Gabriel Barlette. I do not give him other notice than this for two reasons; the first, because there is reason to believe that the sermons which pass under his name are spurious compositions, as indeed is asserted by a cotemporary, Leander Alberti, who says that they were the composition of a pretender who took the name of the great preacher.

It is therefore not fair to judge of a really famous man from works which may not be his. Another reason why I have limited to a few lines my notice of sermons which were undoubtedly popular, if we may judge of the number of impressions they went through, is that there is positively no good to be got from them; they are full of the grossest absurdities and the most profane buffoonery. I have given an account of some three or four of this class of sermon, and I can afford no more room to similar profanities.

Gabriel Barlette was a Dominican, and was born at Barletta in the kingdom of Naples. He lived beyond 1481, for he speaks of the siege and capture of Otranto by Mahomet II. as a thing of the past. In one of the sermons attributed to him is the following passage on the close of the temptations:—" After His victory over Satan, the Blessed Virgin sends Him the dinner she had prepared for herself, cabbage, soup, spinach, and perhaps even sardines."

In a sermon for Whitsun-Tuesday, he rebukes distractions in prayer, and he illustrates them in this unseemly way. He represents a priest engaged at his morning devotions, saying, " Pater noster qui es in cœlis—I say, lad, saddle the horse, I'm going to town to-day!—sanctificatur nomen tuum,—Cath'rine, put the pot on the fire!—fiat voluntas tua—Take care! the cat's at the cheese!—panem nostrum quotidianum—Mind the white horse has his feed of oats. . . . . Is this praying?" No, Gabriel, nor is this preaching!

Another preacher of the same stamp was Menot. Michael Menot was born in Paris; he was a Franciscan, and died at an advanced age in 1518.

Take this specimen of his reasoning—
"The dance is a circular way;
The way of the Devil is circular;
Therefore the dance is the Devil's way."
And he proves his minor by the Scriptural passages "circuivi terram," "circuit quærens quem devoret," "in circuitu impii ambulant." In his sermon for Friday after Ash-Wednesday he thus expresses his sense of the value of magistrates: "Justices are like the cat which is put in charge of a cheese lest the mice should eat it. But if the cat lay tooth to it, by one bite he does more mischief than the mice could do in twenty. Just in the same manner," &c. The following is a specimen of his style, a sad jumble of Latin and French. He is giving a graphic description of the prodigal son wasting his goods. "Mittit ad quærendum les drapiers, les grossiers, les marchands de soye, et se fait accoutrer de pied en cap; il n'y avait rien à redire. Quando vidit sibi pulchras caligas d'écarlate, bien tirées, la belle chemise froncée sur le collet, le pourpoint fringant de velours, la toque de Florence, les cheveux peignés, et qu'il se sentit le damas voler sur le dos, hæc secum dixit: Oportetne mihi aliquid ? Or me faut-il rien? Non, tu as toutes tes plumes; il est temps de voler plus loin. Tu es nimis propè domum patris tui, pro benè faciendo casum tuum. Pueri qui semper dormierunt in atrio vel gremio matris suæ, nunquam sciverunt aliquid, et nunquam erunt nisi

asini et insulsi, et ne seront jamais que nices et béjaunes. Bref qui ne fréquente pays nihil videt."

Of course this sermon was not thus preached, but it gives us an idea of Menot's acquaintance with Latin, and of his utter inability to render the slang which had disfigured his vernacular by classic phrases.

But it must not be supposed that all preachers of the fifteenth century were like these clerical jesters.

Gabriel Biel was grave and dignified, his sermons remarkably simple in construction, and full of wisdom and fervour. The same may be said of Thomas à Kempis, John Turricremata, and Henry Harphius.

With the sixteenth century a new phase of pulpit oratory was about to dawn. Men wearied of conventional restraints, and spoke from the heart, knowledge was profounder, less superficial, the conceits of schoolmen were kept in the background, and scriptural illustrations brought into greater prominence. Anecdote was still used as a powerful engine for good, but it was anecdote such as would edify. Similes were introduced of the most striking and charming character; and the preachers sought evidently rather to instruct their hearers, and to render doctrine intelligible, than to surround themselves with a cloud of abstruse doubts and solutions, to the bewilderment of their hearers, and to their own possible glorification. It is impossible not to see in this a fruit of the Reformation. To people famishing for the bread of life, the preachers of the fifteenth century had given a stone, and now their successors were alive to the fact, and strove earnestly to remedy it. They threw themselves forward like Phineas, and stood in the gap, so that it is to them, perhaps, more than to great theologians like Bellarmin, that the Catholic Church must look with thanks for having stayed the advancing tide of reform.

If, in that age of religious upheaval, the pulpit had remained as unedifying as heretofore, there can be no manner of doubt that the eruption in Germany would have devastated Italy, France, and Spain. Indeed the Huguenot party in France was very powerful, and extended so widely that it must be a matter of surprise to many to find its tenets now represented by a few miserable, quivering fragments. In fact the Roman Church, after the first shock, recovered ground on all sides, for her clergy rose to meet the emergency, and turned to the people as the true source of strength to the Church, and leaned on them, instead of putting her trust in Princes. I cannot believe that the massacres of the Huguenots had any thing to do with the extirpation of Protestantism in France, for persecution strengthens but never destroys. I am rather inclined to attribute it to the vigour with which the clergy of the time set themselves to work remedying the abuses which had degraded pulpit oratory. Sacred eloquence is the most powerful engine known for influencing multitudes, and the Catholic clergy resolutely cultivated it, and used it with as much success as Chrysostom, Gregory, or Augustine. They had a vast storehouse of learning and piety from which to draw, the writings of the saints and doctors of the Church in all ages, and they drew from it unostentatiously but effectively. Their sermons were telling in a way no Protestant sermons could equal, for the Calvinist or Lutheran had cast in his lot apart from the great men of antiquity, whilst the Catholic could focus their teaching upon his flock. The former had but their own brains from which to draw, whilst the latter had the great minds of Catholic antiquity to rest upon. There are vast encyclopedias and dictionaries of theology, moral and dogmatic, filled with matter any Catholic preacher of the meanest abilities could work up into profitable and even striking discourses, great collections of anecdote and simile, which he might turn to for illustrations, and, above all, exhaustive commentaries on every line, aye, and every word of Scripture.

From all these great helps to the preacher, the Protestant minister conscientiously, and through prejudice, kept aloof.

This may account for the undoubted fact that after the first flush of triumph, sacred oratory in the reformed communities sank to as dead and dreary a level as it had attained in the fifteenth century.

The Protestant preachers were not always as grotesque, but they became as dull and unspiritual, whilst the Roman Church having once napped, never let herself fall asleep again, but with that tact which once characterized her, but which is fast leaving her, she stirred up and kept alive ever after the fire of sacred eloquence.

And here I must make an extraordinary statement, yet one indisputably true, however paradoxical it may appear.

The main contrast between Roman Catholic sermons and those of Protestant divines in the age of which I am speaking, consists in the wondrous familiarity with Scripture exhibited by the former, beside a scanty use of it made by the latter. It is not that these Roman preachers affect quoting texts, but they seem to think and speak in the words of Scripture, without an effort; Scriptural illustrations are at their fingers' ends, and these are not taken from one or two pet books, but selected evenly from the whole Bible.

Let me take as an instance a passage selected at hap-hazard from Königstein, an unknown German preacher. He is preaching on the Gospel during the Mass at dawn on Christmas Day. I choose him, for he is as homely a preacher as there was in the sixteenth century, and as he may be taken as a fair representative of a class somewhat dull.

"'And the Shepherds said one to another, Let us now go even unto Bethlehem, and see this thing which is come to pass' (Luke ii. 15). The Saviour being desirous of weaning altogether the hearts of His own people from worldly glory, not only chose to be born in poverty, but to be announced *to* poor folk, and to be proclaimed *by* them. And this He chose lest the beginning of our faith should stand in human glory or wisdom, *which is foolishness with God*, whereas He desired that it should be ascribed to Divine grace only; therefore the Apostle says, '*After the kindness and love of God our Saviour towards man appeared,*' &c. *Kindness and love* in His conversation, and His nativity into this world, by taking our flesh; *of God our Saviour*, by His own vast

c

clemency; *not by works of righteousness which we have done,* for *we were by nature children of wrath,* so that our works were not done in justice, nor could we gain safety by them; but *according to His mercy He saved us* by present grace and by future glory, as *we are saved by Hope;* and it is *He who hath called us with an holy calling, not according to our works, but according to His own purpose and grace, which was given us in Christ Jesus before the world began, by the washing of regeneration and the renewal of the Holy Ghost,* that is, by the washing of Baptism, which is a spiritual regeneration, for, *except a man be born of water and of the Spirit, he cannot enter into the Kingdom of God.* Water cleanses the body without, and the Spirit purges the soul within. In Baptism man ends the old life which *was under the law,* that he may begin the new life which is *under grace;* so that he who believes is daily renewed more and more *by the Spirit, which is given us* in Baptism; as says the Apostle, *Be renewed in the spirit of your mind,"* &c.

Of a similar character are the sermons of Helmesius, and the simple, earnest, and thoughtful postils of Polygranus.

There is another observation which I must make upon these venerable preachers. It is impossible to read them attentively without observing how different in tone they are to modern ultramontane theologians, and how sadly modern Romanism has drifted from primitive traditions, and how rapid has been its descent, when this is noticeable by ascending the stream of time but a few centuries.

I am not prepared to say that there is nothing false and unprimitive in the doctrine of these great preachers, but that doctrinal corruption was not then fully developed. I suppose that an English priest would find it hard to select a sermon of the new Roman school, which he could reproduce in his own pulpit; but if he were to turn to these great men of a past age, he would meet with few passages which he should feel himself constrained to omit. The germ of evil had been slowly expanding through the middle ages; it flowered at the close, and now it has seeded, and become loathsome in its corruption.

Let me take the worship of the Blessed Virgin, which has of late assumed such terrible dimensions. A modern Roman preacher rarely misses an opportunity of inculcating devotion to Mary. But it was not so with the old preachers. They do use language which cannot always be justified, but, more often, language which ought to be frankly accepted by us, considering that the tone of English reverence is unwarrantably low with regard to the blessed ever-virgin Mother. Often when there is a natural opening for some words of deification of Mary, the preachers of the fifteenth, sixteenth, and seventeenth centuries turn from it to make a moral application to their hearers. I will only instance De Barzia, a bishop of Cadiz. He gives three sermons for the Purification.

The first is on the care which a Christian man should take not to scandalize his neighbours by any act which though innocent might give offence, or by the neglect of any duty.

c 2

The second is on the great danger of setting an evil example.

The third is on the funeral taper, by the light of which those truths, which man saw not in the day of his life, are then most evidently discerned.

For the Annunciation he gives three sermons. The first on the modesty of Mary, which all should imitate. The second is on the general confession of sin made in Lent. The third is on the promptitude with which man should act on Divine impulses.

It is true that De Barzia uses strong language from which we should dissent, on the feasts of the Assumption and the Nativity of Mary; but the fact of letting two of her festivals pass without pointing her out as a prominent object of worship is what, I should suppose, no modern Ultramontane would do.

I must now turn to a bright and pleasant feature in these preachers—their keen appreciation of the beauty of nature. This indeed had been a distinguishing characteristic of the Middle Ages. In architecture, in painting, and in poetry, even in preaching, the great book of nature had been studied, and its details reproduced. As the sculptor delighted to represent in stone beast, and bird, and plant; as the painter rejoiced to transfer to canvas, with laborious minuteness, the tender meadow flowers; so did the preacher pluck illustration from the book of nature, or refer his hearers to it, for examples of life.

With the Renaissance, the artist turned from the contemplation of God's handiwork, but not so the sacred orator. In him the same love for the works of God is manifest, his mind returns to them again and again, he gathers simile and illustration from them with readiness and freedom, he seems to stand before his congregation with the written word in his right hand, and the unwritten word in his left, and to read from the written, and then turn to the unwritten as the exponent of the other. Nature was not then supposed to be antagonistic to Revelation, but to be its Apocrypha, hidden writings full of the wisdom of God, and meet "for examples of life and instruction of manners."

The great Bernard used the heart-language of every mediæval theologian when he said, "Believe me who have tried it; you will find more in the woods than in books: the birds will teach you that which you can learn from no master."

In like temper did Philip von Hartung preach to a courtly audience on the text, "Consider the fowls of the air," and drawing them away from the glitter of the palace, and the din of the city, set them down in a meadow to hear the lessons taught them by the lark.

"Consider the fowls of the air, and look first to the lark (*alauda*), drawing its very name, *a laude*, out of praise; see how with quivering wing it mounts aloft, and with what clear note it praises God! Aldrovandus says that he had been taught from childhood, that the lark mounted seven times a day to sing hymns to its Creator, so that it sings ascending, and singing soars.

"St. Francis was wont to call the larks his sisters,

rejoicing in their songs, which excited him to the praise of his Creator. Seven times a day might we too chant our praise to God: first for our creation, which was completed in seven days; then for our Redemption, which was perfected by the seventh effusion of blood; thirdly, for the seven sacraments instituted by Christ; fourthly, for the seven words uttered from the Cross; fifthly, for the seven gifts of the Spirit shed on us from on high; sixthly, for our preservation from the seven deadly sins, even though the just man falleth seven times a day (Prov. xxiv.); and lastly, for the seven sad and seven glorious mysteries of the Blessed Virgin Mary.

"A heavenly lark was royal David, going up to Thee, O God, 'seven times a day' to praise Thee! David from the softness of a palace; David from the cares of a kingdom; David from the tumult of battle; David engaged in so great correspondence with many and mighty kings, seven times a day, rose to the praise of God; and shall not you, my brethren, mount from your case seven times a day to give thanks unto God? Threefold, aye! and fourfold, were our blessedness, if from this vale of tears our hearts would but wing their way on high to seek true and never-fleeting joys. Notice the lark! it is not content, like the swallow, to skim the surface of earth, but it must struggle up higher and higher. 'The higher the soul goes,' says Hugo, ' the more it rejoices in the Lord.' And just as the lark when on earth is hushed, but mounting breaks into joy and song; so does the soul raised to Heaven rapturously and sweetly warble. It sings not upon the topmost boughs of trees, as though spurning all that is rooted in earth. And so do you cast away all cares, all intercourse, all affairs of life, all that is evil, all, in short, that is earthy. Socrates was wont to say that the wings of a lark failed us when we came down from Heaven, drawn by the host of earthly objects. But we can spread them again to flee away and be at rest, if we will, by earnest endeavour, dispose our hearts to mount, and so go on from grace to grace."

Beside this let me place a lesson from the flowers, culled from Matthias Faber. "They teach us to trust in God. I pray you look at Divine Providence exerted in behalf of the smallest floweret. God has given it perfect parts, and members proportioned to its trunk; He has provided it with organs for the performance of all those functions which are necessary to it, as the drawing up of juice, and its dispersion through the various parts; a root branching into tiny fibres riveting it to the soil; a stalk erect, lest it should be stained and corrupted through contact with the earth, strong also, lest it should be broken by the storm, a rind thick or furred to protect it from cold, or heat, or accident; twigs and leaves for adornment and shelter; a most beauteous array of flower above the array of Solomon in all his glory. He has given it, besides, a scent pleasant to beasts or men; He has endued it with healing properties, and, above all, with the faculty of generating in its own likeness. How many benefits conferred on one flower! one flower, I say, which to-morrow is cut down and cast into the oven! What, then, will He not give to man, whom He has made in His own image, an heir of Heaven! . . . 'Consider the lilies of the field how they grow,' aye! *how* they grow, how is it? They grow steadily night and day, stretching themselves out and expanding, so that no man may discern the process going on. So, too, let us grow, daily extirpating vices, daily implanting virtues, thus sensibly increasing, so that, after the lapse of years, we may be found to have advanced in spiritual growth, though we ourselves may not have known it. As said the Apostle, 'Forgetting those things which are behind, and reaching forth unto those things which are before, I press towards the mark' (Phil. iii. 13).

"They teach us, also, to sigh for heavenly beatitude, and the society of the blessed. If even in this world such variety of flowers is seen, such beauty, such fragrance, and these in flowers which to-day are and to-morrow are cast into the oven, what will be the beauty, what the variety, what the glory of the elect in the kingdom of God! Those who go to distant lands are ever discovering fresh and fresh flowers; and so in Heaven is there unmeasured variety among the angels and the elect.

"Yet in all this variety there is perfect unity. For as in the same garden, or meadow, the flowers are content with their several beauties, and no one impedes the growth of another, or thrusts it out of its place, but all look up to the one sun, and bask and grow and gather strength in his brightness; so also in Heaven. There each of the Blessed will be content with his portion of glory, none interfering with another, none envying another. For all will see God face to face, and live and move and have their being in His presence, and therewith be satisfied through eternity."

Simile has been used extensively in all ages of the Church, but in the fifteenth century it had become very mean and coarse. Meffreth could talk of the world as being untranquil, like a globule of quicksilver, never to be brought to rest till fused to a black residuum in the sulphurous blast of Hell; and could illustrate the text, "Here we have no continuing city," by comparing this poor world of ours to the weed-covered back of a large whale, which an eminent and veracious navigator—of course he means Sinbad—mistook for a verdant isle, only to discover his mistake when he began to drive into it the stakes of his habitation.

Far nobler was the use of simile in the great revival of the sixteenth century.

Pre-eminent among those who made it a vehicle for conveying truths, are the names of De Barzia and Osorius; both men of great refinement of taste and richness of imagination.

What, for example, could be more graceful than the following, given by the Bishop of Cadiz, when speaking of the impossibility of man comprehending the reason of God's dealings, when He touches with the finger of death at one time a child, at another an aged man, then a youth, and next, perhaps, one in full vigour of manhood? To us, this selection seems to be a matter of chance, but there is no chance in it. The Bishop then uses this illustration. The deaf man watches the harpist, and sees his fingers dance over the strings in a strange and unaccountable way. Now a strong silver cord is touched, then a slender catgut string. At one time a long string is set vibrating, at another a very short string; now several are thrummed together, and then one alone is set quivering. Just so is it with us; we hear not the perfect harmony, nor follow the wondrous melody of God's operations, for the faculty of comprehending them is deficient in us, and to us in our faithlessness there seems chance and hazard, where really there exists harmony and order.

Osorius uses a different simile in illustrating an idea somewhat similar.

He is speaking to those who murmur at God's dealings in this world, and who would fain have His disposition of things altered in various particulars. He then says, that those who look on an unfinished piece of tapestry see a foot here, a hand there, a patch of red in one spot, of green in another, and all seems to be confusion. Let us wait till the work is complete, and we shall see that not a hand or foot, not a thread even is out of place. Such is the history of the world. We see blood and war where there should be peace; we see men exalted to be kings who should have been slaves, and men condemned to be slaves who would have ruled nations in wisdom and equity, and we think that there is imperfection in the work. Wait we awhile, till at the Last Day the great tapestry of this world's history is unrolled before us, and then we shall see that all has been ordered by God's good providence for the very best.

But Scripture supplied most of the illustrations needed by these preachers. It was to them an inexhaustible storehouse, from which they could bring forth things new and old. Holy Scripture seems to have supplied them with every thing that they required; it gave them a text, it afforded confirmation to their subject; from it they drew mystical illustrations for its corroboration, and examples wherewith to enforce precept.

To some, the sacred page may be crystalline and colourless as a rain-drop, but to these men who knew from what point to view it, it radiated any colour they desired to catch.

They did not always make long extracts, in the fashion of certain modern sermon-composers, who form a sermon out of lengthy Scriptural passages clumsily pegged together, always with wood; but with one light sweep, the old preachers brush up a whole bright string of sparkling Scriptural instances, in a manner indicating their own intimate acquaintance with Scripture, and implying a corresponding knowledge among their hearers. Take the following sentence of an old Flemish preacher as an instance: he is speaking of the unity prevailing in heaven :—

"*There* all strife will have ceased, there all contradiction will have ended, there all emulation will be unknown.

"In that blessed country there will be no Cain to slay his brother Abel; in that family, no Esau to hate Jacob; in that house, no Ishmael to strive with Isaac; in that kingdom, no Saul to persecute David; in that college, no Judas to betray his master."

Let me take another example from a sermon on the small number of the elect.

" 'Many are called, but few are chosen.'

"Noah preached to the old world for a hundred years the coming in of the flood, and how many were saved when the world was destroyed? Eight souls, and among them was the reprobate Ham. Many were called, but only eight were chosen.

"When God would rain fire and brimstone on the cities of the plain, were ten saved? No! only four, and of these four, one looked back. Many were called, but three were chosen.

"Six hundred thousand men, besides women and children, went through the Red Sea, the like figure whereunto Baptism doth even now save us. The host of Pharaoh and the Egyptians went in after them, and of them not one reached the further shore. And of these Israelites who passed through the sea out of Egypt, how many entered the promised land, the land flowing with milk and honey? Two only—Caleb and Joshua. Many—six hundred thousand—were called, few, even two, were chosen. All the host of Pharaoh, a shadow of those who despise and set at nought the Red Sea of Christ's blood, perish without exception; of God's chosen people, image of His Church, only few indeed are saved.

"How many multitudes teemed in Jericho, and of them how many escaped when Joshua encamped against the city? The walls fell, men and women perished. One house alone escaped, known by the scarlet thread, type of the blood of Jesus, and that was the house of a harlot.

"Gideon went against the Midianites with thirty-two thousand men. The host of Midian was without number, as the sand of the sea-side for multitude. How many of these thirty-two thousand men did God suffer Gideon to lead into victory? Three hundred only. Many, even thirty-two thousand men, were called; three hundred chosen.

"Type and figure this of the many enrolled into the Church's army, of whom so few go on to 'fight the good fight of faith!'

"Of the tribes of Israel twelve men only were chosen to be Apostles; and of those twelve, one was a traitor, one doubtful, one denied his Master, all forsook Him.

"How many rulers were there among the Jews when Christ came; but one only went to Him, and he by night!

"How many rich men were there when our blessed Lord walked this earth; but one only ministered unto Him, and he only in His burial!

"How many peasants were there in the country when Christ went to die; but one only was deemed worthy to bear His cross, and he bore it by constraint!

"How many thieves were there in Judæa when Christ was there; but one only entered Paradise, and he was converted in his last hour!

"How many centurions were there scattered over the province; and one only saw and believed, and he by cruelly piercing the Saviour's side!

"How many harlots were there in that wicked and adulterous generation; but one only washed His feet with tears and wiped them with the hair of her head! Truly, 'Many are called, but few are chosen.'"

We hear but little in modern sermons of the mystical

interpretation of Scripture, which was so common in all earlier ages of the Church. The Epistles of St. Paul show us that the primitive Church was accustomed to read Scripture in a mystical way. What, for instance, can be more "fanciful," as we moderns should say, than his allegorizing of the history of Isaac (Gal. iv. 22—31), and of Moses (1 Cor. x. 1), or his argument from the law that the laity should pay for the support of their pastors: "For it is written in the law of Moses, Thou shalt not muzzle the mouth of the ox that treadeth out the corn" (1 Cor. ix. 9, 10), and "Let the elders that rule well be counted worthy of double honour (i.e. *honorarium*, contribution in money) . . . *for* the Scripture saith, Thou shalt not muzzle the ox that treadeth out the corn?" (1 Tim. v. 17, 18.) Bacon said that we should accept as conclusive the meaning of Scripture which is most plainly on the surface, just as the first crush of the grape is the purest wine, forgetting, as Dr. Neale aptly remarks, that the first crush of the grape is not wine at all, but a crude and unwholesome liquor. Certainly modern preachers are ready enough to give us the most superficial interpretation of Scripture, and rarely trouble themselves with probing the depths of Holy Writ for fresh lessons and new beauties. In the same way it was quietly assumed till of late that the ocean below that depth which is storm-tossed was quite azoic. We know now that that untroubled profound teems with varied forms of life, and is glorious with hitherto undreamt-of beauties. Our modern divines are content with the troubled sea of criticism, and pay no heed, and give no thought, to the manifold beauties and wonders of the tranquil deeps of God's mind, above which they are content to toss. The analogy between God's word written and God's unwritten word is striking. Yet we are satisfied to know that the further the great volume of Nature is explored, the closer it is studied, the greater are the wonders which it will display. Why, then, do we doubt that the same holds good with the written word? Deep answers to deep, the deep of Nature to the deep of Revelation. The Same Who is the Author of Nature is the Author of Revelation; and we may therefore expect to find in one as in the other that "His thoughts are very deep," "His ways past finding out;" that in one as in the other there is a similarity, a mighty variety yet an essential unity, a vast diversity yet a perfect harmony; that there are mysteries in both, through which, as through a glass darkly, shines the wisdom of the Creator.

Commentators on Scripture, such as Scott and Henry, really fill pages and volumes with the most deplorable twaddle, and exhibit conclusively their utter incapacity for commentating on any single passage of Scripture. Not only are their comprehensions too dull to grasp the moral lessons in the least below the surface, but they entirely ignore the mystical signification of the events recorded in the Sacred Writings. To the Mediæval divines and those who followed their steps, every word of Scripture had its value; indeed, the very number, singular or plural, of a substantive was with them fraught with significance. Take one instance; Stella the Franciscan remarks, on St. John xiv. 23:—

"'Jesus answered and said unto him, If a man love Me, he will keep My *word* (τὸν λόγον μου τηρήσει): he that loveth Me not, keepeth not My *words* (τοὺς λόγους μου οὐ τηρεῖ).' Love of God makes one command out of many, for to him who loves, the many precepts are but as one. So here Christ says, 'If any man love Me, he will keep My word;' but of him who loves not, He says, 'He keepeth not My words.' Of him who loves, it is spoken in the singular; of him who loves not, in the plural. Eve said, 'Of the fruit of the tree which is in the midst of the garden, God hath said, Ye shall not eat of it, neither shall ye touch it, lest ye die' (Gen. iii. 3); whereas God forbade only the eating, not the touching. But a chilled heart made one command into two; whilst a heart full of love, like that of David, could sum up the six hundred and thirteen precepts of the old law into one, when he exclaimed, 'Thy commandment is exceeding broad,' and 'Lord, what love have I unto Thy law, all the day long is my study in it.'"

Compare with this suggestive passage the only remark made on the text in D'Oyly and Mant: "The manifestation I mean is, that of inward light and grace, which shall never depart from those who are careful to live as I have commanded them." The observation of Stella is suggestive, that in D'Oyly and Mant is decidedly the reverse.

But I would speak now of the mystical interpretations of Scripture. I have only room for a very few. The following are from Marchant. "Unless Christ had been sent, none of us would have been released from our iniquities. Wherefore the Apostle often exhorts the Jews not to glory in the law, for the law did not suffice to justify and to make alive. Do you desire a figure of this mystery? Listen to that of Elisha. He was asked to come and call to life a child which was dead : he sent his servant first with a staff, which he was to lay upon the dead child; but neither servant nor staff were of avail. Then went he himself, and see what he did: 'He went up, and lay upon the child, and put his mouth upon his mouth, and his eyes upon his eyes, and his hands upon his hands:' contracting himself to the form of the child; 'and the flesh of the child waxed warm ... and the child opened his eyes.' You see the figure, attend to the verity. God sent Moses His servant, and the Prophets, with the staff of the law; but neither they nor the law could avail to restore man to life from the death of sin. It was necessary, therefore, that He Himself should go to man, and bow Himself to man by the assumption of man's nature, and contract Himself to the form of a child by the Incarnation, not only casting Himself on this our dead nature, but taking our nature, hands, arms, mouth, and soul to Himself. . . . . This circumstance of the closing of the door that none might see, when Elisha stretched himself upon the child, is not without significance. For as none discerned how Elisha, that great man, was able to contract himself to the form of a little boy; so no one can comprehend how the Son of God, so high and so mighty, could unite, and apply, and abase, His nature to ours; so that He became mortal Who was immortal, passible Who was impassible, infant Who was God. In all these the mystery is great, the door is shut; it is not necessary for us to see, but it is necessary for us to believe. We have another figure in the sign given to Hezekiah. When he was sick unto death, the sun going back ten degrees was the sign of his restoration to health. 'And the sun went back ten degrees on the dial of Ahaz.' In like manner, that man might rise from the sickness unto death of sin, it was necessary that 'the Sun of Righteousness' should descend through the nine angelic choirs, 'being made a little lower than the angels,' as though going down nine degrees till He reached man the tenth."

"The Lord said to Joshua, 'Moses My servant is dead: now therefore arise, go over this Jordan, thou, and all this people, unto the land which I do give them' (Joshua i. 2). Joshua is by interpretation a Saviour, and is the same as Jesus. As he, after conquering Amalek, brought the people into the land of promise, and divided the land between them; so has Christ come to overcome the devil, and to introduce Christians daily into His Church through the Baptismal stream, and finally to lead them into glory. Moses could not bring them in, for the Father saith unto the Son, 'Moses My servant is dead.' The ceremonies of the law are made of none effect, 'now, therefore, arise' from the bosom of the Father, enter the earth in human form, expel the devils: 'go over this Jordan,' drink of the brook of Thy Passion in the way, 'Thou, and all this people,' for by the way by which goes the head, by that must the members go, and where leads the general, there must follow the soldiers, 'and go unto the land which I do give them'—the land of the living, to which Christ ascends and we follow ; to which neither law nor prophets, no nor Moses, could introduce us, but only our Joshua, our Jesus, the Son of God."

I have not yet spoken of the text, except to mention Maillard as having preached on the same throughout a season of Lent. Some of the earlier mediæval preachers delighted in selecting strange texts, and even went so far as to take them from other books than Holy Scripture. Indeed Stephen Langton composed a sermon, still preserved in the British Museum, and published in Biographia Britannica Literaria, on the text :—

> " Bele Aliz matin leva
> Sun cors vesti e para,
> Enz un verger s'en entra,
> Cink flurettes y truva,
> Un chapelet fet en a
> de rose flurie ;
> Pur Deu trahez vus en là,
> vus hi ne amez mie ; "

which was a dancing-song. Maillard also did the same thing when he preached in Thoulouse, singing at the top of his voice as a text the ballad "Bergeronnette Savoisienne."

Peter of Celles took a stanza from a hymn, and his example has been followed by others. Hartung preached from the words, "It fell, it fell, it fell," occurring in the parable of the sower.

Texts have sometimes been selected with remarkable felicity. I have room for two instances only.

In the reign of King James I., a clergyman was to preach before the Vice Chancellor at Cambridge, who was a very drowsy person. He took his text from the twenty-fourth chapter of St. Matthew, "What, can ye not watch one hour?" and in the course of his sermon very often repeated these words, which as often roused the vice-chancellor from his nap, and so irritated him, that he complained to the bishop. The bishop sent for the young man, that he might hear what he had to say for himself in extenuation of the offence; and so well pleased was he with the preacher's defence, that he recommended him to be one of the select preachers before the King. On the occasion of his occupying the pulpit before James (First of England and Sixth of Scotland), he took for his text James i. 6, "Waver not," from the translation then in use. This somewhat startled the King, for it touched him on a weak point; but he loved a joke, and was so well pleased with the preacher's wit, that he appointed him one of his own chaplains. After this the bishop ordered the young man to preach again before his university, and make his peace with the vice-chancellor. He did so, and took for his text, "Whereas I said before, 'What, can ye not watch one hour?' and it gave offence; I say now unto you, 'Sleep on, and take your rest.'" And so left the university. The other story is less known. A Capuchin having to preach one day in a church at—I believe—Lyons, slipped on the steps into the pulpit, and fell on his head. The Franciscan garb is scanty, and the congregation were startled by the apparition of a couple of bare and brawny legs protruded through the banisters. The unlucky preacher however picked himself up with great rapidity, and stationing himself in the pulpit, before the general titter had subsided, gave out his text, selected with great readiness from the gospel for the day—" Tell the vision to no man."

Next to the text in a sermon comes the exordium.

If a royal personage were present, some compliment was expected to be paid by the preacher to his august hearer, at the opening of the sermon. Some of the greatest preachers have injured their reputation by indulging in unmerited flatteries. Chaussemer, a Jacobite, preaching after the famous passage of the Rhine, before Louis XIV. in Holy Week, when according to custom, the king washed the feet of some poor folk, used these words, " The haughty waves of the Rhine, which you, Sire, have passed as rapidly as they themselves are rapid, shall one day be dried up; but these drops of water, which your royal hands have sprinkled over the feet of the poor, shall ever be treasured before the throne of God." Noble was the commencement of a sermon of Father Seraphim, when preaching before the same monarch. "Sire!" he began, "I am not ignorant of the fact that custom requires me to address to you a compliment; I pray your Majesty to excuse me; I have searched my Bible for a compliment,—I have found none." I cannot omit here the really magnificent exordium of a preacher, who, in his matter and style, belonged to the seventeenth century, but who flourished in the eighteenth—I allude to Jacques Brydaine, born in 1701. He had been a mission-preacher in the country, when he was suddenly called to preach at St. Sulpice, before the aristocracy of Paris. The humble country parson, on mounting the pulpit, saw that the church was filled with courtiers, nobles, bishops, and persons of the highest rank. He had been instructed in the necessity of acknowledging their presence by a compliment. But listen to the man of God.

"At the sight of an audience so strange to me, my brethren, it seems that I ought to open my mouth to ask your favour in behalf of a poor missionary, deficient in all the talents you require, when he comes before you to speak of your welfare. But far from it, to-day I feel a different sentiment; and though I may be humbled, do not think for one moment that I am troubled by the miserable anxieties of vanity;—as though, forsooth, I were preaching myself. God forbid that a minister of Heaven should ever think it necessary to excuse himself before such as you! Be you who you may, you are but like me, sinners before the judgment-seat of God. It is then only because I stand before your God and my God, that I am constrained now to beat my breast. Hitherto I have published the righteous dealings of the Most High in thatched temples. I have preached the rigours of penitence to unhappy ones, the majority of whom were destitute of bread. I have announced to the good inhabitants of the fields, the most awful truths of religion. Wretched one that I am, what have I done! I have saddened the poor, the best friends of my God; I have carried terror and pain into the simple and faithful souls which I should have sympathized with and consoled.

"But here, here, where my eyes rest only on the great, the rich, the oppressors of suffering humanity, the bold and hardened in sin; ah! here only is it, here in the midst of these many scandals, that the word of God should be uttered with the voice of thunder; here is it that I must hold up before you, on one hand the death which threatens you, on the other, my great God who will judge you all. I hold at this moment your sentence in my hand. Tremble then before *me*, you proud and scornful men who listen to me. Listen when I speak of your ungrateful abuse of every means of grace, the necessity of salvation, the certainty of death, the uncertainty of that hour so terrible to you, final impenitence, the last judgment, the small number of the elect, hell, and above all eternity! Eternity! behold the subjects on which I shall speak, subjects which I should have reserved for you alone. Ah! what need I your suffrages, which may, perchance, damn me without saving you? God Himself will move you, whilst I, His unworthy minister, speak; for I have acquired a long experience of His mercies. It is He, and He alone, who in a few moments will stir the depths of your consciences."

Passing from the exordium to the subject: that which is so tedious in modern sermons is the want of variety in the matter. There are a stock of subjects of very limited range upon which changes are rung, but these subjects are so few that the changes are small in number. Many years ago I was staying with a relation in holy orders, after a tour through different watering-places. and I mentioned to him the curious fact, that on three consecutive Sundays, in different churches, I had heard sermons on Felix waiting for a more convenient season. Having mentioned this, I forgot the circumstance. Five years after I was in a cathedral town, and went to one of the churches there, on a Sunday morning. To my surprise I saw my relation sail up the nave in rustling silk, preceded by the verger, escorting him to the pulpit. As he passed my pew, our eyes met. He was as surprised to see me as I was to see him, as he was only a visitor like myself. I noticed signs of agitation in his countenance, and that he was some time before he delivered his text, which was upon Zaccheus in the sycamore-tree.

After service I waited for him, and on our meeting, his first words were, "You wretched fellow! You put me terribly out; I had Felix trembling in my pocket ready for delivery; but when I saw you, our conversation five years ago flashed across me, and I had to change the sermon in the pulpit." But this was not all. Next Saturday I was at the other end of England, staying with a country parson, and I related this incident. My host pulled a long face, broke out into a profuse perspiration, and said,—"I am really very sorry, but I had prepared Felix for to-morrow, and what is more, I do not see my way towards changing the subject."

The remarkable part of this anecdote is, that the moral application was similar in all these discourses. Now, the sermons of the divines of the fifteenth, sixteenth, and seventeenth centuries seldom offended in this manner. Matthias Faber published three enormous volumes of sermons for every Sunday in the year, containing some fifteen discourses for each, and they are perfectly varied in matter and in application.

The following is a list of the subjects for one Sunday —the second in Lent:—

St. Matt. xvii. "He was transfigured before them."

Sermon I.—The means whereby a hardened sinner may be transformed into a new man, and his heart be softened.
 1. By constantly hearing God's Word.
 2. By assiduous prayer.
 3. By earnest endeavour.
 4. By diligent practice of virtues.

Sermon II.—The incidents which took place on Mount Tabor, and the lessons they give us.
 1. By labour must we pass to glory, for it was "after six days" and a laborious ascent that the mountain-top was reached.
 2. Beatitude is to be sought above, not on earth, for the disciples were rebuked for desiring to make tabernacles on earth, the true tabernacle being in heaven.
 3. In every act we should consider the end: thus Christ in the glory spoke of His approaching decease.
 4. Those who would see the glory of God must watch.
 5. Christ is to be heard by all, for He is glorified of His Father.
 6. Christ's passion to be constantly before the minds of His servants.

Sermon III.—What might be seen on Mount Tabor.
1. The glory of Christ.
2. Our own future glory, the reflex of His.
3. The vanity of worldly glory.
4. The certainty of future judgment[2].

Sermon IV.—Why Christ in His passion made His decease (*excessum*). The point of this sermon depends on the various significations of the Vulgate expression, *excessus*.
1. He deceased (*excessit*) to show us how great an evil is sin.
2. To show us His fervent love.
3. To compensate for our evil deaths by His most perfect and holy death.
4. To compensate for our defects by His superabundant merits.

Sermon V.—Pious exercises for the season of Lent.
1. The exercise of fasting; set before us by the example of Moses and Elias, each of whom fasted during forty days.
2. The exercise of prayer; set before us by the example of Christ, who was transfigured "as He prayed." (Luke ix. 29.)
3. The exercise of conversion; set before us by Christ's raiment becoming white and glistering; teaching us that we must wash our robes, and make them white in the blood of the Lamb.

---

[2] The manner in which these and other points are deduced from the text cannot be explained here; suffice it to say that it exhibits great ingenuity and subtlety in the preacher.

4. The exercise of making devout use of God's Word; "This is My beloved Son, in whom I am well pleased; hear ye Him."

5. The exercise of the memory of Christ's passion; by the example of Moses and Elias talking with Him of "His decease which He should accomplish at Jerusalem."

6. The exercise of present opportunities of grace, before the cloud obscures Christ, and ye desire "to see one of the days of the Son of Man, and shall not see it."

Sermon VI.—The transfiguration of Satan into an angel of light, and how he deceives men.

1. He leads them into the high mountain of pride, that thence he may cast them down.
2. He dazzles by the splendour of his countenance.
3. He puts on a show of virtue, like glistering raiment.
4. He brings upon men a cloud of doubts and difficulties and worldly delights.
5. From that cloud he utters a loud voice, filling men with fear at the difficulties besetting them if they would begin the service of God.
6. He chooses his apostles.
7. He produces Elias; example of indiscreet zeal.
8. He brings forward Moses; example of exaggerated meekness.

Sermon VII.—Eternal good things offered us by God: what they are and what their nature.

1. They are solid and true. For the transfigura-

tion was not a mere dreaming vision, but seen when the three "were awake."
2. They are pure and sincere; unmixed with care, or pain, or toil.
3. They are secure and stable.
4. They are perfect and complete.
5. They are realities, not promises.
6. They are bought at a low price.

Sermon VIII.—Wherefore Christ was transfigured.
1. To establish our faith in the resurrection.
2. To excite our hope.
3. To kindle our love.
4. To console the Church.
5. To show who He was.
6. To teach us to despise the world.
7. To give a moment's joy to His body, wearied with fasting, watching, and toil.

Sermon IX.—The great Parliament held on Tabor, and what was treated of there.
1. The death of Christ was discussed.
2. The glory of Christ the Mediator and Legislator.
3. The imperial laws were drawn up; that
   α. The cross should precede the crown;
   β. The end should be held ever in view;
   γ. Beatitude should be sought above;
   δ. The passion should ever be had in remembrance.

Sermon X.—On the meaning of *excessus*.

Sermon XI.—Man's fourfold transfiguration.
1. From a state of grace into one of sin.

2. From a state of sin into a state of grace.
3. From the state of delight in this world into the misery of hell.
4. From the state of pain here to the glory of Heaven.

Sermon XII.—The five sources of joy to the redeemed.
1. The place—Heaven.
2. The society of the blessed.
3. The delights of the senses, especially of the eyes and ears.
4. The dowers of the risen body; glory, agility, subtlety, and impassibility.
5. The beatific vision of God.

Sermon XIII.—The estimation in which indulgences are to be held.

Sermon XIV.—Lessons drawn from the Gospel.
1. The power of prayer.
2. The duty of watching.
3. The image of worldliness in Peter, to be avoided.
4. The lightest sins to be shunned.
5. The difference in the falls of good and bad.
6. The fleeting nature of joy here on earth.
7. The signs of Christ's coming in judgment.

Sermon XV.—Mysteries contained in the Gospel.
1. Why Christ elected only three of His disciples.
2. Why He led them into a mountain apart.

3. Of the nature of the Transfiguration.
4. Why Moses and Elias appeared.
5. Why they spoke of the passion.
6. Why the cloud overshadowed the vision.
7. Why the disciples were bidden to be silent respecting the vision.
8. How the Father is well pleased in the Son.
9. The order of events in the Transfiguration.

These sermons of Matthias Faber, and indeed most of the sermons of great preachers in the sixteenth and seventeenth centuries, are very simple in construction. The system of dividing into a great number of heads, and then subdividing, had been cast aside by the Catholic preachers at the Reformation, as unprofitable. But Protestant orators continued the baneful practice. It prevailed till lately in England, and is common still in Scotland. Dr. Neale remarks, "One would think, to read some of the essays written on the subject, that the construction of a sermon was like a law of the Medes and Persians. Look at Mr. Simeon's one-and-twenty tedious volumes of 'Horæ Homileticæ.' The worthy man evidently considered this the greatest system of divinity which English theology had ever produced. And of what does it consist? of several thousand sermons treated exactly in the same ways, in obedience to precisely the same laws, and of much about the same length. Claude's Essay had laid down certain rules, and Simeon's Discourses were their exemplification. . . . The preacher opens with a short view of the circumstances under which the text was spoken. This is a very convenient exordium, because it fills two or three pages with but little trouble. The clergyman has only to put Scripture language into his own, and he is fairly launched in his sermon without any effort. Another almost equally easy method of opening is to be found in drawing a contrast between the person or thing of which the passage in hand speaks, and that to which the writer may wish to allude. And it has this special advantage; that if he is unlucky in finding much likeness between the two, he is sure to discover a good deal of *un*-likeness, and either treatment will supply a good number of words. Thus, as every one knows, come the heads,—a most important part in this style of discourse. Taking Mr. Simeon as a pattern, we shall find that they cannot be less than two, nor more than four; though, indeed, there are not wanting those who have greatly extravagated beyond the superior limit, as the Puritan divine's 'And now, to be brief, I would observe eighteenthly, that—' so and so, may suffice to prove. Then come all the minutiæ of subdivisions and underdivisions (little heads, as the charity children call them), all set forth, when the aforesaid discourses came to be printed, in corresponding variations of type." After a lengthy exordium, one Sunday evening, a preacher divided his subject into twenty heads, each of which he purposed D.V. considering in all its bearings. On hearing this, a man in the congregation started up and proceeded to leave the church, when the preacher called to him, "Wherefore leave, friend?" "I am going for my nightcap," replied the man; "for I plainly see that we shall have to pass the night in church."

The conclusion in an old sermon of the three centuries under review, is short, pithy, and to the purpose. It consists in a vehement appeal to the consciences of the hearers, in the application of a parable or a Scriptural illustration, in a rapturous exclamation to God in the form of a brief extempore prayer, or in a string of anecdotes and examples. The following is a conclusion by Guevara, Bishop of Mondoneda :—

"Tell me, O good Jesu, tell me, is there any thing in a rotten sepulchre which is not in my sorrowful soul and unhappy life? In me more than in any shall be found hard stones of obstinacy, a painted sepulchre of hypocrisy, dry bones of old sins, unprofitable ashes of works without fruit, gnawing worms of great concupiscence, and an ill odour of an evil conscience. What, then, will become of me, O good Jesu! if Thou do not break the stones of my faults, throw down the sepulchre of my hypocrisy, reform the bones of my sins, and sift the ashes of my unruly desires? Raise me up, then, O good Jesu! raise me now up: not from among the dead which sleep, but from among sins which stink, for that the justification of a wicked man is a far greater matter than the raising up of a dead man ; because that in the one Thou dost use Thy power, and in the other Thou dost exert Thy clemency."

Many of Paoletti's sermons conclude with a string of incidents and stories, from which I presume any preacher using the sermon might select that which seemed to him most appropriate.

The effect produced by the sermons of these ancient preachers was sometimes extraordinary. Jerome de

Narni preached one day before the Pope, with such zeal, on the duties of residence, that next day, thirty bishops fled from Rome to their several dioceses. St. John Capistran, a Franciscan, preached in 1452 at Nuremberg, in the great square of the town, and he spoke with such vehemence against gambling, that the inhabitants brought out their dice, cards, and tables, heaped them up and burned them before him. The same thing happened next year at Breslau. Of the marvellous conversions, the result of their powerful preaching, of course we can know but little, though there is evidence that they were neither few nor unenduring. It was not an uncommon thing for people to throw themselves at the foot of the pulpit, and denounce themselves of crimes they had committed, or to throng the preacher after the sermon was over, earnestly desiring him to hear their confessions. But the most original scene, the result of a sermon of great power, exhorting to confession and amendment, took place in a church at Turin, during Lent in 1780. After the most touching appeal of the preacher, a man stood up and began to confess his sins aloud. He said that he was a lawyer, and that his life had been one of extortion. He mentioned the names of several families which he had pillaged, widows' houses he had devoured, orphans' substance which he had conveyed into his own pocket. This went on for some little while, when suddenly a gentleman on the other side of the church sprang up, and in a voice choking with rage, exclaimed, "Don't believe him! it is not true. The good-for-nothing fellow is describing me and my acts; but I never did any thing of the kind!" It was evident to all that the cap fitted.

The story is told of a rich usurer of Vicenza urging the ecclesiastical authorities of the town to send for an eminent preacher to declaim against usury. "He has converted many usurers in various towns of Italy," said the man, "and I should not in the least scruple to pay some of the expense of his coming here." "But," said the clergyman to whom he spoke, "if you are determined on your own conversion, you surely need not the exhortations of a preacher to strengthen your resolutions." "Oh!" replied the usurer, "it is not for myself. This town is so full of usurers, that there is no room for a poor fellow like me to gain a livelihood. Now if they were all converted, and gave up their evil habits, there would be some chance of my being able to pick up a living."

There were, indeed, preachers who were sent round the country to declaim against certain special sins. Their *forte* lay in attacking one species of guilt, but they were ineffective when preaching on another point. There were preachers whose strength lay in panegyrics upon saints; and others who—I pity them—were great in funereal discourses. Of the latter class was Geminiano, a Dominican, whose "sermones funebres" were published at Antwerp in octavo, 1611. They are ninety-eight in number. He preached over the graves of popes, archbishops, bishops, abbots, soldiers, doctors, rich men and beggars, beautiful women, an emperor, a drowned man, a prisoner who died in jail, an executed criminal, and a murdered man or two; he preached at the interment of merchants, fishermen, ploughmen, and huntsmen—in short, it would be hard to find some over whom John Geminiano did not dolorously hold forth. A sad moment for Geminiano when he first let people understand that his strong point lay in a grave.

A really great preacher was never suffered to hide his light under a bushel; according to our parochial system, the most eloquent man of the day may, for aught we know, be perched on the top of a Wiltshire down, or be buried in the clay of a North Devon parsonage, fifteen miles from a railway.

The Roman Church had the regular clergy to draw upon for preachers, and as they had no ties, could send them up and down the country, so that the same course of sermons would serve them again and again. Indeed, otherwise it would have been impossible for some of the favourite preachers to have continued providing fresh matter and committing it to memory, for it must be remembered written sermons are not tolerated in the Roman communion. It might be possible for an eloquent man with a lively imagination to continue for long without exhausting himself, but how could a solid and learned preacher, who relied on quotations, continue extracting and committing to memory long paragraphs from the Fathers, Sunday after Sunday, and year after year? Let us take a sermon of Mangotius the Jesuit, for instance.

Adrian Mangotius was a Dutchman, and consequently eminently practical and unimaginative. His sermons are good in their way; there is not a bit of originality in them, but the fragments of which they are composed are judiciously selected. In his fifty-ninth discourse, he quotes St. Matthew four times, St. Luke thrice, St. John twice, the Epistles five times, Revelation once, the Old Testament ten times, St. Augustine a dozen times, St. Gregory four times, St. Ambrose twice, St. Jerome twice, St. Bernard twice, St. Thomas Aquinas once, Cicero some three or four times, Plutarch, Sallust, and Virgil once.

This style of sermon suits some people, perhaps, but it did not take with the masses, who liked richness of imagery, abundance of simile, and neatness of illustration. So when Father d'Harrone, a man of sound learning, but little brilliancy of genius, preached a course in Rouen, after the great Bourdaloue, to use his own words:—"When Bourdaloue preached last year at Rouen, artisans quitted their business, merchants their wares, lawyers the court, doctors their sick; but as for me, when I followed, I set all in order again; no one neglected his occupation."

In the following pages I have given a sketch of some of the most remarkable preachers of the fifteenth, sixteenth, and seventeenth centuries. The divine and the bibliographer may miss the names of some great and eminent men, as Paolo Segneri, Antonio Vieyra, Latimer, Andrewes, &c. But these men are either well known, or their lives and sermons are within the reach of English readers. Segneri's Lenten sermons have been translated and somewhat diluted by Prebendary Ford, Vieyra is noticed in "Mediæval Sermons," and English preachers I have omitted entirely to notice, because they are for the most part hopelessly dull.

# GABRIEL BIEL.

This excellent and learned man is generally supposed, from his name Biel, the modern Bienne, to have been a Swiss, though some assert that he was a native of Spire, and the latter is probably the real place of his nativity, though his family may have been of Swiss extraction, for he is called " Gabriel Biel ex Spira " in the beginning of his " Sermones de tempore," as published by Johan Otmar, in Tubingen, 1510.

He went by the name of "the Collector," from the fact of his being a laborious compiler rather than an original composer.

He was undoubtedly one of the best scholastic divines of his age, and was a careful reader of the Fathers.

Gabriel Biel was a member of the Regular Canons, and was Doctor of Theology, which he taught as professor in the University of Tubingen, founded by Count Eberhardt of Wirtemberg, in 1477.

He soon became a favourite with this nobleman, who listened to his sermons with delight.

At one time he was vicar and ordinary preacher at the metropolitan church of St. Martin at Mainz, but the date of his appointment is uncertain. Gabriel Biel was a man of gravity and learning; his sermons were popular, not on account of the eloquence with which they were delivered, for of that there was little, but of their beautiful simplicity and intrinsic excellence.

His hearers were not amused by his discourses, but I venture to say that they were edified.

His style is pithy, his sentences pregnant with meaning, for what he said, he said in few words, and he said it too very gracefully. Instead of wearying his hearers with unprofitable scholastic quibbles, he gave them practical good advice in plain and homely words.

The date of his death is not known with certainty, but it probably took place in 1495, though, according to some, he lived till 1520.

His works and their different editions are:—

Commentaria in libros iv. Magistri Sententiarum; Basil., 1512; Brixiæ, 1574, 5 vols. in 3, 4to.

In Sententias; Parisiis, 1514, fol.; Basileæ, Joc. de Pfortzen, 1512, 2 vols. fol.; Lugduni, Jacobus Myt, 1527, fol.

Sententiarum repertorium generale; Lugduni, Cleyn, 1614, fol.

Historia Dominicæ Passionis, prodiit una cum Defensorio et Sermonibus cunctis; Hagenæ, 1519.

Passionis Dominicæ sermo historialis; sine loco et anno, 4to.

Sermones dominicales de tempore. Sermones de festivitatibus Christi. Absque loci et anni nota, 4to.; sine loco impressionis, 1494, fol., Goth., a 2 col.; Tubingen, Otmar, 1510, Goth., 2 col.; Haguenaw, 1515, 4to.

Sermones de Sanctis. Absque loci et anni nota, 4to.
Ejusdem de festivitatibus Virginis Mariæ, 1599, 4to.
Sermones sacri totius anni; Brixiæ, 1583, 4to.
Sermones medicinales contra Pestem et Mortis Timorem; Defensorium obedientiæ pontificis. Expositio canonis Migsæ; Lugduni, 1514, fol.; Parisiis, Jehan Petit, 1516, fol., Goth.; Hagenoiæ, 1519, fol.; Antuerpiæ, 1549, 8vo.; Lugduni, 1542; Venet., 1576; Brixiæ, 1580; Bergomi, 1594.

Lectura super canonem Missæ, in alma universitate Tuwingensi ordinarie lecta; Reutlingæ, Otmar, 1488, fol.

Tractatus de Monetarum potestate simul et utilitate; Norembergiæ, 1442, 4to.; Colon., 1574, 4to.; Lugduni, 1605, 4to.

Epitome scripti Gulielmi de Occam, et Collectorium circa iv. libr. Sent. Still in MS.

The Exposition of the Mass which passes under the name of Biel is really a copy from the work of Eggeling of Brunswick, as, indeed, Biel owns at the end of the book.

The simple earnestness of Gabriel Biel renders his sermons very attractive; and as being the production of a well-read and a thoughtful man, these sermons furnish ample material for reproduction in the modern pulpit. The reader will not find in Biel much of the fire of the Italian pulpit, nor the richness of simile which characterized the Spanish preachers, but he will find plain truths drawn from Scripture in a very straightforward manner, and applied in short but nervous sentences.

Perhaps the main difference between a sermon of

Biel and one of a modern preacher, is, that the former contains many thoughts in few words, whilst the latter consists of many words, but contains few thoughts.

Analysis of Sermon xix. "De tempore," being a sermon for Septuagesima, on the text from the Gospel: "The kingdom of heaven is like unto a man that is an householder, which went out early in the morning to hire labourers into his vineyard," &c. (Matt. xx. 1.)
Introduction.
> Hitherto the Church has been keeping festival. Now she closes her season of festivity, that she may lament and weep for the lapse of her sons.
> A. (1) Man's *nature* as it left the Creator's hands was very noble. It was immortal, not by nature, but by grace. By nature it was capable of decay and death, but by grace it was provided with the tree of life, the fruit of which renovated and preserved it.
> (2) Man's *life* was maintained subject to a condition, the condition of obedience. Its preservation was contingent on the keeping of God's commandment.
>> The soul as created was innocent; man was wise in intellect and clean in affections; he was associated with angels, accustomed to converse with God, peaceful in conscience, and endowed with all gifts of nature and grace.
> (3) Man's *knowledge* of God was not enigmatical, but intuitive. He saw God by some internal

power of contemplation : a power not so perfect as that will be which we shall possess in our country, nor so imperfect as that which we have in the way.

(4) Man's *conscience* was at peace with God; and internal peace implies external peace as well. Paradise was a place of perfect peace, for the elements were tranquil, the animals were in subjection, nourishment was in abundance.

Had this state of peace continued, man would not have died, but he would have been translated to Heaven without death.

(5) But alas! all this was forfeited by sin; and man was spoiled of his graces, and wounded in his faculties.

He lost original righteousness, and with its loss his tranquillity was disturbed, his flesh became unbridled, his intellect parched, his will depraved, his memory disturbed.

(6) Creation was moreover armed against him, so that earth was no more ready to nourish him spontaneously; but he was constrained to labour in the sweat of his brow for his daily bread.

B. And now we are led to a consideration of the Gospel for the day, which speaks of fallen man, and of fallen man working, and working moreover to recover the conditions which he had before he fell.

The Gospel is full of doctrine and dogma suited to all conditions of men.

Doctrine I. is serviceable for increasing our faith. For the Gospel teaches us that in no other way can we attain the reward of the kingdom, than by working with true faith in the Lord's vineyard, which is the Church.

It is not sufficient that we should be called, we must work as well.

Work is not sufficient, unless it be work in the Lord's vineyard.

Work in vineyards of our own planting will never be paid for by the Lord of the vineyard, when He comes to give the labourers their hire.

Again; this Gospel opposes the presumption of those carnally-minded men who think to be saved by faith only; whereas faith without works is dead, being alone.

Doctrine II. giveth hope. For it shows that the kingdom of Heaven is open to all, and closed to none; all are called to the work, even though it be at the last hour. So long as there is life there is hope.

Again; this Gospel, at the same time as it shows that none should despair, opposes all sloth and cowardice in undertaking the work of the salvation of the soul.

Doctrine III. inflames charity. For it exhibits to us in a remarkable manner the love of the Father towards man; a love which embraces all, and rejects none; a love ready to reward both the righteous and the unrighteous, both the good and the bad, if the unrighteous and bad will but turn from their evil ways, and be converted, that He may heal them. Examples of those called at late stages of life, and yet meriting a reward equal to those who have borne the burden and heat of the day, are afforded by David, St. Peter, St. Paul, St. Matthew, and St. Mary Magdalen.

Again; by this Gospel all excuse is removed from those who neglect the work of their salvation, for no man can say that he has not been hired, inasmuch as God calls him throughout life; calling him externally and internally,—externally, by the beauty of creation, by the Holy Scriptures, by preaching, by the scourge of afflictions; internally, by shame at sin committed, by fear occasioned by the knowledge of the uncertainty of the hour of death, by dread of judgment, by horror of hell, by promises of absolution, of glory, and by aspirations of love for the mysteries of Redemption.

Doctrine IV. induces to humility. For it shows us that no man should puff himself up with spiritual pride, because he may have laboured long in his Lord's vineyard, or may have been kept free from falling into heinous crimes; by this Gospel he is taught that many that are first shall be last, and the last shall be first. "Why dost thou judge thy brother? or why dost thou set at nought thy brother? for we shall all stand before the judgment-seat of Christ."

"Therefore judge nothing before the time, until the Lord come, who both will bring to light the hidden things of darkness, and will make manifest the counsels of the hearts; and then shall every man have praise of God."

Doctrine V. urges to the fear of God, lest by delay in undertaking the work of his conversion, man should neglect the call of God to work, and lest he thereby lose his hire.

"Let him that thinketh he standeth, take heed lest he fall." "Watch ye, therefore, for ye know not when the Master of the house cometh, at even, or at midnight, or at the cock-crowing, or in the morning: lest coming suddenly, He find you sleeping."

Conclusion. Finally, let all keep in mind the awful sentence of Him who cannot err: "Many are called, but few are chosen." Let each fear for himself, lest he be found among the number of the called who have neglected the vocation; and let him strive by all means in his power to be of the number of the chosen.

This sermon is followed by another on the same Gospel; the subject being, the small number of the elect.

The analysis given will show how wholesome and practical were the discourses of this truly pious and learned man.

# JEAN RAULIN.

JOHN RAULIN, born at Toul in 1443, of noble and wealthy parents, was educated at the Navarre College in Paris, and took honours in theology in the year 1479.

In 1481 he was elected President in the place of William de Châteaufort, and he filled the position with the utmost probity, and ruled with singular discretion.

In 1497 he resigned the mastership and retired to Cluni, where he lived a life of great sanctity.

In 1501 he obtained a commission from Cardinal Ambassiani to introduce a reform into the Benedictine Order. He died at Paris in the Cluniac monastery, on February 6th, 1514, aged seventy-one.

Raulin was a man of considerable piety, of blameless life, and of the utmost integrity. He seems to have been regarded in his day as a great preacher, and his sermons have been several times republished. Those for Advent have passed through six editions, and those for Lent through five.

Besides sermons, he wrote a " Doctrinale " on the

triple death,—the death of the body, the death in sin, and the last or eternal death. He is also the author of a volume of letters and tracts on the reform of the Cluniacs; also of "The Itinerary of Paradise," "A Discourse on the Reformation of the Clergy," and a "Commentary on Aristotle's Logic."

He was a dry and methodical preacher, vehement in his denunciations of the corruptions in Church and State, and ready unscrupulously to attack all abuses in ecclesiastical discipline. His style is wholly devoid of eloquence, and is precise and dull. His sermons are full of divisions and subdivisions, which could never have fixed themselves in the minds of his audience, and serve only to perplex his readers. They are wanting in almost every particular which would make a sermon tolerable now-a-days; and after a lengthened perusal, one rises from the volumes wondering how there could have been found hearers to listen to such discourses, or readers sufficiently numerous to necessitate a rapid succession of editions.

As a representative man of a type common enough in the century which produced him, he is valuable. For the age and the taste of his period, he is grave; but he sometimes sinks almost as deep in buffoonery as Menot, Meffreth, or Oliver Maillard.

As an example, taken at hazard, of one of his sermons, I will give a short outline of his Epiphany discourse on the text—"It is the Lord that commandeth the waters; it is the glorious God that maketh the thunder; it is the Lord that ruleth the sea." (Ps. xxix. 3, 4.)

Question. Was it of necessity that Christ should be baptized?

Answer. No; for reasons taken from St. Bernard and St. Chrysostom.

Christ however consented to be baptized for three reasons,—

1. To set an example to us.
2. To conceal Himself from Satan, who beholding Him baptized might hesitate to regard Him as the Messiah.
3. To show His perfect humility.

In the baptism of our Lord, there were three manifestations: the Son in His humanity, the Father by the voice, the Holy Ghost by the descent of the dove.

Then follows an exhortation to humility, and a warning to priests and people to practise godliness instead of contenting themselves with professing it. "The hand is bigger than the tongue," hints Raulin.

The Son was manifest in His humanity. A question is asked:—Did John Baptist recognize Christ?

Answer:—

1. He recognized Him when He was unborn, "The babe leaped in my womb for joy;" but he did not distinctly know Him now, for—the reason given is perfectly monstrous—Aristotle says that the human frame changes every seven years.
2. He knew that Christ was among the throng by a sort of inspiration, but he knew not which of his hearers was Christ.
3. Knowledge is double; it arises out of

    *a.* Demonstration, and is acquired by reason.
    β. Experience.

Raulin investigates the knowledge of John, and resolves the question by stating that at first he had no certain knowledge, but that after the manifestations accompanying the baptism, he obtained it by experience.

A second question is asked:—Why St. John Baptist did not venture to touch Christ?

Answer:—

1. Because he had an instinctive fear of God present in the flesh.
2. Because he was conscious of his own sinfulness.

The Father was manifest by the voice.

In holy baptism all men are made in like manner children of God. We are made children,

1. By adoption—to the Father.
2. By ingrafting—to the Church.
3. By spiritual generation—to the priest who baptizes.

From this arises the question:—Did St. John the Baptist become spiritual father of our Lord by baptizing Him?

This Raulin answers in the negative; for,

1. Christ received not grace through the ministration of John; for He was full of grace from the moment of His conception.
2. The rite was imperfect.
3. It was a baptism of repentance, which could not avail spiritually one who had never sinned.

The Spirit was manifest under the form of a dove.

The dove appeared above water, and here follows a dissertation on the virtues of divers waters.

The question arises:—Why did the Spirit elect the form of a dove?

This Raulin answers in the following manner:

1. A dove is without gall, and is harmless, and therefore represents the character of those born of the Spirit.
2. A dove bore the olive-branch to the ark, in token of God being reconciled. And by baptism we are reconciled to God.
3. A dove has seven qualities, resembling the Spirit's sevenfold gifts. These are,—

(1) It moans instead of warbling; this represents the spirit of holy *Fear*.

(2) It is a gentle bird, and is offered in sacrifice; thus representing the spirit of *Piety*.

(3) It is granivorous, not carnivorous; thus it shadows forth the spirit of *Knowledge*.

(4) It dwells in the clefts of the rock; thus exhibiting the character of the spirit of *Fortitude*.

(5) It brings up the young of others; thus showing forth the spirit of *Counsel*.

(6) It rends not what it eats, but swallows whole; a type of the spirit of *Understanding*.

(7) It dwells beside waters; thereby exhibiting the marks of the spirit of *Wisdom*.

All these points are drawn out at length, and examined minutely; Scripture is tortured to illustrate them, and illustrations of a most unsuitable nature are brought to bear upon them.

It will be seen from this abstract, how thoroughly unprofitable the sermons of Jean Raulin prove to be; they bear the character of playing and trifling with Scripture and with the most sacred subjects, and it is sad to think that a good and blameless man, such as he was, should have degraded the ministry of God's Word to a mere tissue of Sunday puzzles.

Raulin delighted in far-fetched similes, and in tracing out types beyond all limits of endurance. That of the dove was sufficiently extravagant, but what can we say to his working out the details of the parable of the Miraculous Draught of Fishes, in such a manner as to make the little fishes resemble the faithful in the Church, because,

> (1) Fish have their eyes at their sides, and so can always see about them; and faithful Christians are ever watchful.
> (2) Fish advance in the water by wagging their tails; and good Christians have to advance by remembering the end of all things!!
> (3) Little fish are eaten by big fish, and so of the faithful it is said, "Men shall devour you."

Occasionally Jean Raulin tells a story to enliven his discourse—stories in the pulpit were in vogue then—and these anecdotes and fables are often exceedingly good and pointed, but they are most unsuited to a sermon.

On one occasion, when preaching on the corruptions in the Church, and declaiming against the way in which the clergy condoned moral sins of the blackest dye, but showed the utmost severity when the slightest injury was done to the temporal welfare of the Church, he illustrated his subject by a story to this effect:

The beasts were once determined to keep Lent strictly, and to begin by making their confessions. The Lion was appointed confessor. First to be shriven came the Wolf, who with expressions of remorse acknowledged himself a grievous sinner, and confessed that he had—yes, he had—once eaten a lamb.

"Any extenuating circumstances?" asked the Lion.

"Well, yes, there were," quoth the Wolf; "for the mother who bore me, and my ancestors from time immemorial, have been notable lamb-eaters, and 'what's born in the bone comes out in the flesh.'"

"Quite so," said the confessor; "your penance is this,—say one Pater Noster."

The next to approach the tribunal of penance was the Fox, with drooping tail, a lachrymose eye, and humble gait.

"I have sinned, father!" began Reynard, beating his breast; "I have sinned grievously through my own fault; I—I—I—yes, I once did eat a hen."

"Any extenuating circumstances?" asked the Lion.

"Two," replied the penitent; "I must say, the fault was not quite my own. The hen was grossly fat, and it roosted within reach. Now, had she been an ascetic, and had she gone to sleep in some tree, I should never have touched her, I assure you, father."

"There is some truth in that," said the confessor; "say as penance one Pater Noster."

Next came the Donkey, hobbling up to the confessional, and her broken ee-yaws! could be heard from quite a distance. For some time the poor brute was so convulsed with sobs that not a word she said could be distinguished. At last she gulped forth that she had sinned in three things.

"And what are they?" asked the Lion gruffly.

"Oh, father! first of all, as I went along the roads, I found grass and thistles in the hedges; they were *so* tempting that—that—that—ee-yaw, ee-yaw!"

"Go on," growled the Lion; "you ate them; you committed robbery.—Vile monster! I shudder at the enormity of your crime."

"Secondly," continued the Donkey, "as I came near a monastery one summer's day, the gates were wide open to air the cloisters; impelled by curiosity, I—I—I—just ventured to walk in, and I think I may have somewhat befouled the pavement."

"What!" exclaimed the confessor, rising in his seat, and shaking his mane; "enter the sanctuary dedicated to religion—*you*, a female, knowing that it is against the rules of the order that aught but males should intrude; and then, too, that little circumstance about the pavement! Go on," said the Lion grimly.

"Oh, father!" sighed the poor penitent; "the holy monks were all in chapel, and singing the office. They sang so beautifully that my heart was lifted up within me, and at the close of a collect my feelings overcame me, and I tried to say Amen; but produced only an ee-yaw! which interrupted the service and hindered the devotion of the monks."

"Horrible!" cried the Lion, his eyes flashing with pious zeal, his hair bristling with virtuous indignation. "Monster steeped in crime, is there any penance too great to inflict on you? I—" The reader may guess what became of the helpless beast.

This story, which I have related in my own words, instead of giving a literal translation, must have been a cutting satire on the practices of the clergy of that period, and as true as it was cutting; but the pulpit was not the place for it.

Another of Raulin's beast fables is good. It occurs in a sermon on St. Nicolas. He is speaking of the persuasion which parents have that their children are perfect spiritually and corporeally. Once an old toad had a son who was fond of church-going—so fond, indeed, that in the ardour of his devotion he went one day without his socks. This troubled the old toad, as his son was liable to colds in the head if he caught chills in his feet. Seeing the hare dashing by, he called out, "Hey! you, there! going to church, I suppose? Do me a good turn and take my son his socks, or he'll get his death of cold."

"But how am I to know your son?"

"Nothing more easy," replied the toad; "there's not such a good-looking fellow in the crowd."

"Ah! I know him," said the hare; "we call him the swan."

"Swan!" expressed in a tone of contempt, "swan! a fellow with great splay feet and a neck you might tie in a knot!"

"Well, let me see! I know him; he is the peacock."

The toad screamed with dismay. "How can you insult me by thinking that cracked-voiced thing my son?" and he puffed himself up to the shape of a ball.

"Then how am I to know your son?"

"Why, look you," pumped forth the toad with stateliness, "he is remarkably handsome—ahem! he is the image of me: has goggle eyes, a blotched back, and a great white belly!"

Now, could any congregation hear this story from the pulpit without laughing? It is sufficiently *piquant*, and would go home to many parents present.

There is a capital story which I believe originated with Raulin, but which has since been versified by Southey, and even dramatized; but it may be questioned whether any modern author has told it with any thing like the *naïveté* of the original.

It occurs in the third sermon on widowhood. I give it in the Latin of the period.

"Dicatur de quâdam viduâ, quod venit ad curatum suum (à son curé), quærens ab eo consilium, si deberet iterum maritari, et allegabat quod erat sine adjutorio, et quod habebat servum optimum et peritum in arte mariti sui.

"Tunc curatus: 'Bene, accipite eum.'

"E contrario illa dicebat: 'Sed periculum est accipere illum, ne de servo meo faciam dominum.'

"Tunc curatus dixit: 'Bene, nolite eum accipere.'

"Ait illa: 'Quid faciam? non possum sustinere pondus illud quod sustinebat maritus meus, nisi unum habeam.'

"Tunc curatus dixit: 'Bene, habeatis eum.'

"At illa: 'Sed si malus esset, et vellet mea disperdere et usurpare?'

"Tunc curatus : 'Non accipiatis ergo cum.'

"Et sic semper curatus juxta argumenta sua concedebat ei. Videns autem curatus quod vellet illum habere et haberet devotionem ad eum, dixit ei ut bene distincte intelligeret quid campanæ ecclesiæ ei dicerent, et secundum consilium campanarum ipsa faceret.

"Campanis autem pulsantibus, intellexit juxta voluntatem suam quod dicerent: 'Prends ton valet, prends ton valet.' Quo accepto, servus egregie verberabit eam, et fuit ancilla quæ prius erat domina.

"Tunc ad curatum suum conquesta est de consilio, maledicendo horam quâ crediderat ei. Cui ille: 'Non satis audisti quid dicant campanæ.'

"Tunc curatus pulsavit campanas, et tunc intellexit quod campanæ dicebant: 'Ne le prends pas, ne le prends pas.' Tunc enim vexatio dederat ei intellectum."

In an Easter sermon, Raulin asks why the news of the resurrection was announced to women. And he replies that they have such tongues that they would spread the news quickest.

He then says that it has been asked why women are greater chatterboxes than men. And the reason he gives is certainly original, if perhaps not conclusive.

Man is made of clay, woman of bone—the rib of Adam. Now if you move a sack of clay, it makes no noise; but, only touch a bag of bones, and rattle, rattle, rattle, is what you hear.

This remark is also made by Gratian de Drusac in his Controverses des Sexes masculin et féminin, 1538, p. 25.

A story told by Raulin, with which I shall conclude, is not without beauty.

A hermit supplicating God that he might know the way of safety, beheld the Devil transformed into an angel of light, who said, " Your prayer is heard, and I am sent to tell you what you must do to be saved ; you must give God three things united—the new moon, the disc of the sun, and the head of a rose." The hermit was nearly driven to despair, thinking that this was an impossibility, but a real angel appeared to him, and told him the solution. "The new moon is a crescent, that is to say a C; the disc of the sun is an O; and the head of a rose is R. Unite these three letters, and offer to God COR, your *heart*, then the way of salvation is open before you."

# MEFFRETH.

According to a mediæval legend, an evil spirit once entered a monastery, passed his novitiate, and became a full brother. In preaching one Advent to the assembled friars, he spoke of the terrors of hell, and depicted them most graphically, being, of course, eminently qualified for so doing. His discourse produced a profound sensation among his audience, their blood curdled with horror, and some of the weaker brethren fainted away. When the true character of the friar was discovered, the Superior expressed to him surprise at his want of judgment in preaching a powerful sermon, calculated to terrify the hearers from ever venturing on the road which leads to the place described by the preacher with such fidelity: but the devil replied with a hideous sneer, "Think you that my discourse would prevent a single soul from seeking eternal damnation? Not so; the most finished eloquence and the profoundest learning are worthless beside one drop of unction,—*there was no unction in my sermon.*"

Meffreth, the subject of this notice, was a preacher of great popularity in the fifteenth century; his sermons display great power of a certain order. He was undoubtedly an accomplished theologian, a good scholar, and a man of diversified reading; he could speak with force, and describe with considerable graphic power,— but for all this, in his two hundred and twenty-five sermons there is not one in which the unction necessary for the conversion of souls is to be discovered. It is quite impossible to read these sermons without feeling that the preacher's great object has been the exhibition of his own ingenuity and learning, not the saving of the souls of his hearers.

Of the man himself but little is known, and that little we gain from his own title-page. From it we ascertain that he was a German priest of Meissen, and that he flourished about 1443.

His only work is the Hortulus Reginæ, seu Sermones Dominicales et de Sanctis, per totum annum, in Partes Æstivalem et Hyemalem distributos. Proderunt Norimbergæ, 1487, fol.; Basileæ, 1488, 2 vols. fol.; Coloniæ, 1645, 4to.; the same sermons, Pars Hiemalis; sine loco et anno, folio.

Sermones de Præcipuis Sanctorum Festivitatibus; Monachii, 1614, 4to.; Coloniæ, 1625, 4to.

Meffreth having stated boldly, in his Sermons on the Conception of the Blessed Virgin, that she was born with the taint of original sin, his editors were put to some trouble in order to get a licence to publish; in the first edition there is an explanatory note by the publisher, in the second, a long preface by Fr.

Joannes de Lapide, a Carthusian and Doctor of the University of Paris, refuting the opinion of Meffreth on this head, and stigmatizing it as heresy, not, however, on Scriptural and Patristic authority, but on the ground of the judgment of Sixtus IV., the decision of the University of Paris, and the decree of the Council of Basle.

The edition of 1625 contains another " Præmonitio ad lectorem, in tres sequentes sermones de gloriosæ Virginis Mariæ conceptione," which, after giving an account of the indulgence decreed by Sixtus IV. to all those who should keep the octave of the feast of the Conception, concludes with these words : " Sixtus Popa IV. constituit, ut nec affirmantes, nec negantes Beatam Virginem sine originali peccato conceptam fuisse, hæreseos, vel peccati mortalis damnarentur, idque Concil. Trident. sess. 5 de peccato originali et Pius V. in quadam sua constitutione confirmarunt: ceterum doctrina dicentium, B. Virginem cum peccato originali fuisse conceptam, pietati ædificationique populi minus videtur profutura. Quare quæ per tres sequentes sermones a Meffreth in hanc sententiam dicuntur, non sunt pro concione rudibus proponenda, sed Doctorum disputationi relinquenda : præsertim cum ex iis quædam admodum incerta et falso quam vero propriora sunt."

Notwithstanding that a *soupçon* of heresy might be supposed to attach to Meffreth by vehement adherents of the dogma of the Immaculate Conception, the man is quite extravagant enough in his teaching about Our Lady to satisfy on all other points the most zealous

Mariolater. For instance, with him, Mary is the garden of all delights (De Sanctis 3), by her name devils are put to flight (48), no one can be saved without her assistance (87 and 95), and she was conceived without earthly father (17). If Meffreth could swallow so many camels, he need not have strained at a solitary gnat. The sermons of Meffreth occupy 1412 pages of small, close print, in double columns, in the edition of Anthony Hierat, 1625; and they are furnished with three indices, one to each of the parts.

They are quite incapable of being reproduced in a modern pulpit, but they are nevertheless valuable, and worth the few shillings which they cost, for Meffreth was a man well versed in the mystical signification of Scripture, and he has carefully gathered together a vast amount of serviceable material, though he has been unable to build it together, with the wood, hay, stubble, which he has added, into a homogeneous mass.

His sermons open with a fact (?) from natural history, to which he gives an allegorical interpretation. This serves as an introduction. The body of the discourse is separated into two or three parts, and each part contains several heads ; each head is again broken into divisions, and each division is subdivided. The sermons vary in length ; those for Saints' days are short, but the rest are of intolerable length. They are enlivened with anecdotes, sometimes good, generally pointless, occasionally absurd.

Those of Meffreth's sermons which are intended as expositions of our Lord's parables are better by far than the rest, and will be found useful by the theological student. As an example, take the following analysis of his exhaustive exposition of the parable of the Sower.

He explains it "anagogicè," "allegoricè," and "moraliter." I shall give only the first two interpretations, as the moral signification has been given in the Gospel, and Meffreth does little else than repeat it.

I. Anagogicè—
  1. God the Father sows seeds of two kinds:
    A. Angelic nature, sown in the beginning,
      α. On the way; i. e. on Christ, its true resting-place, from which some of the angels were snatched away by pride.
      β. On the rock; i. e. on Christ. On this rock Satan fell and was broken. This is the rock which at the last day will fall on him and grind him to powder.
      γ. Among thorns; i. e. envy and ambition.
      δ. On good ground; this is the angelic nature, which rested unfallen on the good ground of God's presence, and there ripened into the fruits of love, reverence, and obedience.
    B. Human nature, sown on the sixth day of creation. This fell—
      α. On the wayside of luxury: for the woman saw that the tree was good for food and pleasant to the eyes.
      β. On the rock of pride: for Eve was tempted by the promise, "Ye shall be as gods."
      γ. Among the thorns of ambition: for the woman saw that the fruit was good to make

one wise, and she desired "to know good and evil."

2. God the Son went forth from the bosom of the Father to sow Himself—
   A. In the womb of the ever-blessed Virgin, that good ground where He would spring up and bear an hundredfold. In her womb He sowed—
      a. His Divinity.
      β. The humanity of Adam's flesh.
      γ. The human soul, which is the breath of God.
   B. When He left the womb of Mary He went forth to sow—
      a. The Gospel, which fell—
         1. On the wayside of the impenitent.
         2. On the rock of Pharisaic pride.
         3. Among the thorns of worldliness and avarice.
         4. On the good ground of the elect.
      β. That He might sow His Divine grace.
      γ. That He might sow His mercy, pardoning iniquity: and this fell—
         1. On the wayside of luxury.
         2. On the rock of despair.
         3. Among the thorns of riches.
   C. His own self did our Lord sow in His double nature, when He left earth for Heaven, there to sow the roses of martyrdom, the violets of confessors, and the lilies of virgins.

II. Allegoricè—
   A. The sower is a preacher of the Gospel. The

seed is the word. The resemblances are sixfold.

α. The seed attracts the moisture of the earth, without which it is sterile.
β. The seed occupies the place of weeds.
γ. It generates seed in its own likeness.
δ. It contains within itself the principle of life.
ε. It is in a state of continual progression; first the seed, then the blade, then the ear, and afterward the full corn in the ear.
ζ. It multiplies itself.

B. The sower is a preacher; his characteristics should be—
1. Discretion as to *where* he sows.
2. Discretion as to *when* he sows.
3. Discretion as to *how much* he sows.
4. Discretion as to *what quality* he sows.

He must also *go forth*—
α. From evil communications.
β. From covetous desires, lest—
  1. His example injure.
  2. His eye be darkened.
  3. He forget his vocation.
γ. To contemplation.

C. The soil is fourfold in its quality.
1. It is trodden down by the continual passing to and fro of worldly and carnal lusts.
2. It is stony, without depth of conviction.
3. It produces thorn-like pleasures, riches, ease, ambition, and luxury.
4. It is good and deep.

Perhaps one of the most striking of Meffreth's sermons, and one free from his worst defects, is that on the text, "A certain man made a great supper, and bade many," &c.; being part of the Gospel for the second Sunday after Trinity. It is divided into three parts, the first two of which I give in abstract, as they are suggestive and beautiful.

By way of introduction, Meffreth observes that Isidore in his Natural History asserts that the tiger is a beast swift as an arrow, marked and dappled with diverse colours, and when it approaches fire or water, or a looking-glass, it becomes so sluggish that it either falls into the fire and is burned, or tumbles into the water and is drowned, or remains in a brown study in front of the mirror till the hunters capture it.

Now this has its moral significance, observes the preacher, for all human beings are tigers, set like arrows to fly swiftly to their true end and aim, eternal happiness, which they would reach, were it not for certain fires and waters and mirrors which retard them, and allow them to fall into the hands of the devils, who are the hunters.

Meffreth having proved that man's true end and aim is eternal beatitude, shows how that he is checked, and falls short of his aim, by the fires of evil concupiscence, the water of impure affections, and the mirrors of worldly felicity. It will be seen that there is some confusion in metaphor here.

Meffreth having settled the tigers, approaches the text.

The supper, he observes, has two significations;

it is (A), the Blessed Sacrament, and it is (B), the beatitude of eternal fruition, the one being the earnest of the other.

And first, with regard to the Blessed Sacrament, he shows that the name of supper applies well to it for three reasons—the first being that it was instituted at the Last Supper; secondly, that cœna is derived from the Greek κενόν, "*new*," and so exhibits it as a sacrament of the New Testament; and thirdly, because κενόν signifies *shadow*, the eucharistic symbols being shadows of the living realities they contain.

A certain man, in the parable, made a *great* supper: a great supper indeed is the Holy Eucharist; great because of the glorious nature of the food; great because of the abundance of meats it offers; these meats being remission of sin, mitigation of carnal desires, a revivification of good works by the destruction of sins, a fructification of virtues, an increase in grace, a mystical ingrafting into Christ, and a pledge of eternal life. Each of these seven meats is treated of at some length, and ramifies into collateral subjects. Great, too, is the supper of the Holy Eucharist, because of its durability. The feast of Ahasuerus, remarks Meffreth, lasted but seven days (Esther i.), whereas that of the Eucharist had lasted 1496 years, that being the date of his sermon. The preacher then, following St. Ambrose, shows who are those who come not to the Holy Table; they are the heathen, the Jews, and the heretics. The heathen, like him who had bought a piece of land, have set their affections on this earth, and sold all that they might secure it. The Jews, ever ploughing with the five yoke of the Pentateuch, never sow in the seed of the Word. The heretic, wedded to a sect of his own choosing, deserts the Catholic Church, which is the Bride of Christ. None of these men, says our Lord, shall taste of My supper.

But secondly (B), the supper signifies the beatitude of celestial glory. The whole of this division is worked out, I think all will agree, with singular felicity.

A supper, to be really great, says Meffreth, must have ten properties or requisites:—

1st. It must take place at a suitable time, neither too early nor too late. That of Ahasuerus was made in the third year of his reign, and that of Christ in the third age, the age of grace.

2nd. It must take place in a spacious, and suitable, and secure spot. That of Ahasuerus was made "in the court of the garden of the king's palace: where were white, green, and blue hangings, fastened with cords of fine linen and purple to silver rings and pillars of marble." And the preacher shows how that the place of the heavenly banquet excels that of Sushan in spaciousness, suitability, and security.

3rd. There must be great liberality and hilarity of the host. Of Ahasuerus it is said, "The heart of the king was merry with wine, and he commanded— to bring Vashti the queen before the king with the crown royal, to show the people and the princes her beauty: for she was fair to look on." Christ also shows His liberality and hilarity by making His feast known to all; by the greatness of His preparation; by His inviting many; by His distress at the refusal of those first invited, and His sending into the streets and lanes of the city; by His compelling men to come in from the highways and hedges.

The fourth requisite of a great supper is the abundance and the variety of the dishes. King Ahasuerus gave drink "in vessels of gold (the vessels being diverse one from another), and royal wine in abundance, according to the state of the king." In like manner has Christ prepared abundance of good things for His marriage supper. And chief among these are the twelve refections of the just, each of which Meffreth comments upon with great beauty. I can but name them.

1. Health without infirmity. (Ps. ciii. 3. Isa. lx. 18.)

2. Youth without age. (Ps. ciii. 5.) This is followed by a dissertation on the apparent age which the resurrection body will have.

3. Satiety without distaste. (Isa. xlix. 10. Eccles. i. 8.) Followed by a proof that the soul can be satisfied with nothing short of God.

4. Beauty without deformity. (Matt. xiii. 43. Wisd. iii. 7.) Followed by a dissertation on the degrees of glory hereafter.

5. Impassibility with immortality. (Isa. xxv. 8; xlix. 10.)

6. Abundance without want; to this the preacher applies very beautifully the text, Judges xviii. 10.

7. Peace without break.

8. Safety without fear. (Ps. cxlvii. 14.)

9. Knowledge without ignorance. (1 Cor. xiii. 12.)
10. Glory without shame. (Col. iii. 4.)
11. Joy without sadness: joy in having overcome our foes, joy in having become purged from every defect, joy in having escaped the woes of the lost.

12. Liberty without restraint, arising from the spirituality of the body. To will being then to do: the spiritual body being capable of travelling as swiftly as mind, of executing whatever the imagination can conceive.

Each Person of the ever-blessed Trinity, observes Meffreth, will grant us three gifts.

God the Father will present us with the unutterable contemplation of His unveiled presence, with the entire possession of all good things, and with the fulfilment of every desire.

God the Son will afford us clean and renewed flesh, sanctified souls radiant with beauty, and participation in the Divine nature.

God the Holy Ghost will give us the sweetness of eternal fruition, the wine of perennial gladness, and the fruits of love, joy, peace, &c. (Gal. v. 22, 23.)

Meffreth then returning to the requisites of a feast, says that the fifth is the courtesy of the ministers. In that made by King Ahasuerus, it is expressly said, "The king had appointed to all the officers of his house, that they should do according to every man's pleasure." How fully will that requisite be obtained in the heavenly banquet! exclaims Meffreth, when even Christ "shall gird Himself and make" His servants "sit down to meat, and will come forth and serve them." (Luke xii. 37.)

The sixth requisite of a feast is sweet music, and here Meffreth speaks of the music of the heavenly city as heard by St. John in Patmos.

The seventh requisite is abundance of light, and on this he quotes the Apocalypse xxi. 23, "And the city had no need of the sun, neither of the moon, to shine in it: for the glory of God did lighten it, and the Lamb is the light thereof."

The eighth requisite is the delicacy of the victuals, and this he applies to the varied delights the redeemed will have in the society of the saints and of the angels in their differing orders and ranks.

The ninth requisite is duration. The banquet of Ahasuerus lasted but seven days, whilst that of Christ will be for ever and ever.

And lastly, a feast must be peaceful and calm. When Ahasuerus made his banquet, he prepared "beds of gold and silver, upon a pavement of red, and blue, and white, and black marble." How much sweeter will be the rest of the redeemed in the green pastures of Paradise, beside the ever-flowing waters of comfort!

In another sermon on the same Gospel, Meffreth strangely inverts the subject just given, and makes the certain man to be the devil, and he describes with equal power the great feast of emptiness which he prepares. The properties of a feast are of course in this case wanting in every particular. For abundance of light there is outer darkness; for sweetness of music there are never-ending cries of despair; for calm and tranquillity there is strife and discord, and instead of those who are at that fearful feast having delicacy or variety of food, they are themselves the food on which the never-dying worm so sweetly feeds.

The commencement of the second sermon for the same Sunday after Trinity is so thoroughly characteristic of Meffreth's worst style, that I must give it in his own Latin.

"Experientia, quæ est rerum magistra,"—note this pompous and stately beginning, and see what it introduces—"sæpe ostendit, quod mus, quandoque intrat promptuarium macilentus, ibique invenit lardum, carnes vel caseum et hujusmodi (and all that sort of thing) comedit, et impinguatur, cumque dominus venit quærens murem, vult fugere per foramen arctum, per quod intravit, sed præ pinguetudine non potest exire, sicque capitur et necatur.

"Moraliter. Per mures hic ad præsens intelliguntur homines, quia, sicut mus ab humo dicitur, eo quod ex humore terræ nascatur. Nam humus terra dicitur. Sic enim homo ab humo est dictus, eo quod *de limo terræ est formatus.* Gen. i." After a few words about minding earthly things, and a quotation from Boetius, he continues,—"Si enim inter mures videres unum aliquem, jus sibi atque potestatem præ cæteris vendicantem, id est, usurpantem super alios mures. O quanto movereris cachinno, id est, risu, quia derisibile esset, et talis potestas terrena scilicet derisibilis, quæ non extendit se ad corpus. Quid vero si tu corpus spectes hominis, quid est imbecillius, id est, debilius homine? quasi diceret, nihil; quos scilicet homines muscarum sæpeque morsus in secreta, id est;"—another id est, Meffreth is intent upon being intelligible,—" in interiora hominis quæque reptantium, id est, serpentium, necat introitus." The construction of this sentence is very confused. " In quo declarat, quod homo est mure debilior, imo parvissimo mure, quia musculus est diminutivum a mure. Iste quidem homo ad instar muris macilentus et nudus intrat in promptuarium hujus mundi. Juxta illud Job i. *Nudus ingressus sum in hunc mundum et nudus revertar illuc.* Cui alludet Apost., 1 Tim. vi., *Nihil intulimus in hunc mundum, haud,* id est, non *dubium, quia nec auferre quid possumus.*"

Having brought us into the larder of this world, Meffreth ought to have followed out the moral application, but he becomes apparently lost over the " lardum, carnes vel caseum et hujusmodi," and never leaves them throughout his sermon.

An Advent discourse opens with the following statement: "Naturalists say that the Balustia, a certain flower of the pomegranate, is cold and dry, and has astringent and stiptic properties, wherefore it is used against dysentery and bloody flux of the stomach. It also restrains choleric vomiting, if it be cooked in vinegar and laid upon the collar-bone—so say medical men."

" Expert naturalists say that every irrational animal, when it feels itself becoming weak and helpless, at once seeks a remedy for its languor, which may restore it to health. .... In like manner, says Isidorus (lib. xii.), stags, when they feel themselves burdened with infirmity, snuff the serpents from their holes with the breath of their nostrils, and having overcome the noxiousness of the poison, reinvigorate themselves with their food. Aristotle (lib. vi.) says of animals, that bears are wont to eat crabs and ants for medicinal purposes. Avicenna relates in his book viii. of animals, that it was related to him by a faithful old man, that he had seen two little birds squabbling, and that one was overcome; it therefore retired and ate of a certain herb, then it returned to the onslaught; which, when the old man observed frequently, he took away the herb. Now when the birdie came back and found it not, it set up a great cry and died. And Avicenna says, 'I inquired the name of the plant, and conjectured it to be of the species which is called *Lactua agrestis.*'" (Dom. Sexagesima i.)

"The owl at night eats the eggs of the jackdaw, because it is strongest by night. But, on the other hand, the jackdaw walks off with the owl's eggs by day, and eats them, because the owl is feeble by day. In like manner the devil devours all man's good works in the night of sin, .... and just as the devil like an owl destroys man's good works by mortal sins, so on the other hand ought man in the day of safety and grace to destroy the devil's eggs by works of repentance." (Feria, 4to. post, Reminiscere i.)

"According to naturalists, salt has the property of preserving from putrefaction. For we see that if meat is placed at full moon in the beams of the moon, it breeds worms, because the moon augments the moisture of the meat, and by this means predisposes it for corruption. If, however, meat is salted, the moon cannot do it so much harm; for salt extracts from the flesh its juices, wherefore men desirous of preserving meat from putrefaction put it in the pickle-tub. Morally—by salt understand the bitterness of penitence, or satisfaction; and by the meat understand carnal delights," &c. (Domin. 2da p. Pascha, 9.)

I have mentioned the fact of Meffreth using stories in his sermons. They occur very frequently; they are not all either appropriate or edifying. The following, however, is pretty: it is to be found in the first sermon on the parable of the Rich Man and Lazarus. Meffreth is speaking of wealth and its cares as contrasted with the *insouciance* of poverty. He then relates the story of a certain Robin, or Rubinus, a poor man who lived under the steps leading into the palace of a wealthy nobleman. Poor Robin had a hard time of it: he toiled all day, and at nightfall he would go about the streets with an old fiddle, playing for a few coppers: sometimes, however, he would get as much as five pence, and then he would fiddle and sing at night on his straw, so cheerily that the rich man in his palace heard him and sighed, because his own heart was never glad. One day the lady of the house said to her lord, "How is it that you with all your wealth are never happy, whilst poor Robin under our stairs is as cheerful as a cricket?" " I will destroy his mirth," replied the rich man; and he secretly conveyed a bag of money into Robin's den.

No fiddle, no song, were heard for many days, for the poor fellow was gloating over his strangely-acquired wealth, and fearing hourly lest it should be taken from him. "How is it," asked the lady of the house, "how is it that Robin neither fiddles, whistles, nor sings now?" "Mark!" replied her lord; "I will restore his song to him." So he reclaimed his money. Now when Robin was free of this source of care, he caught up his fiddle and sang to it right lustily half the night through.

Another charming story told by Meffreth is this:—

There was once an aged hermit in the Egyptian desert, who thought it would be well with him if he had an olive-tree near his cave. So he planted a little tree, and thinking it might want water, he prayed to God for rain, so rain came and watered his olive-tree. Then he thought that some warm sun to swell its buds would be advisable, so he prayed, and the sun shone out. Now the nursling looked feeble, and the old man deemed it would be well for the tree if frost were to come and brace it. He prayed for the frost, and hoar frost settled that night on bar and beam. Next, he believed a hot southerly wind would suit his tree, and after prayer the south wind blew upon his olive-tree and—it died. Some little while after, the hermit visited a brother hermit, and lo! by his cell-door stood a flourishing olive-tree. "How came that goodly plant there, brother?" asked the unsuccessful hermit.

"I planted it, and God blessed it, and it grew."

"Ah! brother, I too planted an olive, and when I thought it wanted water I asked God to give it rain, and the rain came; and when I thought it wanted sun, I asked, and the sun shone; and when I deemed that it needed strengthening, I prayed, and frost came—God gave me all I demanded for my tree as I saw fit, yet is it dead."

"And I, brother," replied the other hermit, "I left

my tree in God's hands, for He knew what it wanted better than I."

Very different is Meffreth's story of the fat priest who was carving a capon in Lent, when his servant burst out laughing behind his back. "Sirrah! what are you laughing at?" asked the globular parson.

"Oh, your reverence! excuse me, but I could not help thinking what a lot of drippings there would be from you, when hereafter the devils have the roasting of you."

# MATTHIAS FABER.

MATTHIAS FABER was born at Neumarkt, in Bavaria, in the year 1586. He was appointed to the cure of the parish of St. Maurice in Ingolstadt, and to the professorship of the University in that town. Whilst there, he published three volumes of sermons for every Sunday in the year, and these have gone through six editions.

He was much regarded as a preacher, and deservedly so, for he was a man full of learning and genius, though not remarkable for his eloquence.

In the year 1637, at the age of fifty-one, he was received into the Society of Jesus at Vienna, and continued after his reception to preach with considerable success. He then published another volume of sermons for all the Sundays and the principal festivals of the year. This book, divided into two parts, is called the Auctuarium, and was thenceforward published along with the former volumes. The Concionum opus tripartitum, together with the Auctuarium, contain one thousand and ninety-six sermons. Besides these, he preached funeral and marriage orations, published after his death, which took place on the 26th of April, 1653, at Tyrnau.

It is not to be expected that in such a vast collection all should be of equal merit; and yet few of Faber's sermons would be put down as bad. The vast majority of them are remarkably good, and full of matter. Not one, perhaps, could be found which does not contain more suggestive remarks than we are accustomed to hear from the modern pulpit in a month. Faber is brief, but what he says he has thought well over, and it is always worth the hearing. He is almost too brief sometimes, for he throws out a brilliant remark, and goes on to another without making the most—without, indeed, making any thing of the former.

How great is the contrast between him and a modern preacher, who every Sunday labours through a polished and carefully worded essay, containing in many words the feeblest whiff of an idea! And Faber could vary his matter to suit his hearers. Preaching before his University, he discussed learned questions in Divinity with great lucidity; but preaching to the good citizens of Ingolstadt, he confined himself to practical instructions.

His style is dignified and earnest, but it is not eloquent, though many of the passages in his sermons are very graceful. And he is perfectly free from the bombast which supplied the place of eloquence among certain preachers of his day.

Matthias Faber does not shrink from telling a story, and a story with a good practical moral to it, but he does not attempt simile to any extent.

There is an apparent crudity in his discourses. Probably this is owing to their being printed from the abstract which he drew up before preaching; so that when delivered, the apparent abruptness and ruggedness of this outline may have been smoothed away.

Few ancient preachers would be more serviceable to a clergyman of the present day, or more acceptable to an English congregation. Unfortunately, the volumes are somewhat scarce, and consequently expensive.

The following is a list of Faber's works and their several editions:

1. Controversiæ contra Altorfienses Professores.
2. Concionum opus tripartitum; Ingolstadii, 3 vols. fol., 1631; Cracoviæ, 1647.
3. Auctuarium Operis Concionum Pars; Græcii, fol., 1646; Antverpiæ, 2 vols. fol., 1647.

Auctuarium pro Dominicis et Sanctis; Cracoviæ, fol., 1647.

Opus Concionum, Pars Hiemalis; Antverpiæ, 3 vols. fol., 1650.

Auctuarium; Antverpiæ, fol., 1653.

Opus Concionum....cum Auctuario; Coloniæ Agrippinæ, 4to., 5 partes, 1669.

Opus Concionum, Pars Æstivalis; Antverpiæ, fol., 1663.

Opus Concionum; Coloniæ, 3 vols., 4to., 1693.

Concionum Sylva nova, seu Auctuarium. Cui accedunt Conciones Funebres, Nuptiales, et Strenales posthumæ. Coloniæ, 4to., tomus primus, 1695.

4. R. P. Matthiæ Fabri Conciones Funebres; Brugis, 12mo., 1723.
5. Höret den Sohn Gottes; Olivæ, 24mo., 1678.

I shall give the reader the outline of some of Matthias

Faber's sermons, that he may judge for himself whether he deserves the praise I have accorded to him.

Fourth Sunday in Lent.

St. John vi. 13. "They gathered them together, and filled twelve baskets with the fragments of the five barley loaves."

Introduction.
There were twelve baskets full of food gathered from this feast which Jesus made in the wilderness, and twelve are the wholesome lessons which I gather from it, and with which I feed you to-day.
1. Learn fervour and zeal for hearing the Gospel.
"The people," we are told, "ran afoot out of all cities, and outwent them, and came together unto Him." Behold their earnestness, and contrast it with your indifference. They came on foot, they came long distances, they came in great numbers, they outwent Christ and His Apostles, they came voluntarily and without having been summoned, they came oblivious of their bodily wants, bringing with them their wives and children. Faber draws a contrast between these people and his hearers, undoubtedly just, but certainly not flattering: and he applies to the latter the words of God to Ezekiel, "Ye pollute Me among My people for handfuls of barley, and for pieces of bread."

2. Learn the various effects produced by God's Word on different hearers.

Faber is singularly infelicitous in filling this basket. He observes that our Lord at one time drew near to the sea, but did not enter it; at another put off a little from land, but soon returned to it, and now in to-day's Gospel crosses the sea, and having crossed it, performs the miracle: so does He shadow forth three kinds of Christians in His mystical Body, the Church: those who only approach the bitter sea of repentance, those who just enter it and again return to land, and those who traverse it and are found meet to sit down in green pastures at His heavenly banquet.

3. Learn the custody of the eyes.

Christ "lifted up His eyes" and beheld the multitude. He had them before on earth, not straying hither and thither; and so He teaches us to restrain our wandering gaze. His eyes meekly rested on earth; Eve's, straying among the boughs, saw the fruit of the tree of the knowledge of good and evil, and those wandering eyes brought death into this world. So did the restless eyes of Potiphar's wife light on Joseph, so did the unguarded eyes of David fall on Bathsheba, and the curious eyes of the two elders on Susanna. But we are not required to keep our eyes always fixed on earth, or closed; but to restrain them from idle curiosity, to avert them from dangerous objects, and to guard them carefully when we pray. There are, on the other hand, times when we should raise them, after the example of Christ. For the considering and relieving of the poor (John vi. 5), in giving thanks (Mark vi. 41), in praying (John xvii. 1), in giving instruction (Luke vi. 20), in seeking the glory of God in all our actions (John xi. 41).

4. Learn to ask God's blessing on your food.

As Christ gave thanks, and looking up to Heaven blessed the loaves and fishes.

We have the same lesson in Deut. viii. 10, "When thou hast eaten and art full, then thou shalt bless the Lord thy God." And we have the example of the Israelites who would not eat of the victims till Samuel had blessed them.

5. Learn care for the poor.

Christ gave the loaves and fishes to His disciples to distribute among the multitude, and so He gives the rich their abundance, not for them to consume it themselves, but that they may "distribute and give to the poor."

6. Learn to see God's providence in the support of all men, and especially of His own servants.

Thus did God provide manna for the Israelites in the wilderness (Exod. xvi. 12), bread and meat for Elijah during the famine (1 Kings xvii. 4), food for Daniel in the lions' den (Bel and Dragon, 33).

7. Learn to seek the food of the soul before seeking that of the body.

Thus Christ before feeding the multitude "spake unto them of the kingdom of God" (Luke), "began to teach them many things" (Mark).

8. Learn that fasting precedes festival, Lent goes before Easter.

So now Christ retired to the wilderness, as "the Jews' passover was nigh at hand; and many went out of the country up to Jerusalem before the passover, to purify themselves" (John xi. 55.)

9. Learn moderation and frugality in diet.

Christ performed the miracle of feeding five thousand, not with luxuries, but with plain and wholesome food, to teach us not to care about luxurious living, but to be content with simple diet.

10. Learn that there should be order in the Church.

For the people sat not down till commanded, and then, not in confusion, but in ranks.

11. Learn to avoid waste, and what is superfluous learn to give to the poor.

This may be gathered from the fragments being collected by the Apostles at Christ's express command.

12. Learn to despise worldly honours.

For when the multitude would have taken Jesus by force, and made Him a king—as we read in to-day's Gospel—He fled from them into a high mountain apart

Conclusion.

Let all who have been fed from these fragments of instruction be satisfied, and, thanking God, acknowledge Christ for their true king.

First Sunday after the Epiphany.

St. Luke ii. 51. "His mother kept all these sayings in her heart."

Introduction.

In God's Word we find rules of life for all conditions of men, for all stages of life, for all positions in society. The Gospel for this day gives instruction to several grades of men.

1. Parents are taught:—
    α. To train their children in the fear and admonition of the Lord. To bring them at an early age to the house of God, to teach them to love its courts, to take pleasure in its services, and to delight in the instructions given there.
    β. To seek their children when they wander from the paths of righteousness, to seek them sorrowing, and to find no rest till they see them restored.
2. Children are taught—
    α. To follow God rather than man; to obey Him in preference to their earthly parents, remembering that "He who loveth father or mother more than Me, is not worthy of Me."
    β. But in every thing else, except where the will

of parents clashes with the will of God, cheerfully to submit to them.

3. Married persons are taught to feel for each other, and to sympathize with each other. Thus Joseph entered into the grief of Mary at the loss of her Son, and returned with her to Jerusalem in quest of Him. And Mary showed deference to her husband, saying, "Thy father and I have sought Thee sorrowing," placing Joseph in honour before herself.

4. Kinsfolk and acquaintance are taught that they have a responsibility in the children of their relatives. Mary and Joseph sought Jesus among them. So God required Abel at the hand of Cain. So the Apostle writes to Timothy, "If any man provide not for his own (i. e. look not after his own), and specially for those of his own house, he hath denied the faith, and is worse than an infidel."

5. Priests are taught to abide in the temple, and to be ready to hear the doubts and perplexities of others, and to answer them as God gives them understanding.

6. Finally, all may learn—
   *a.* From the fact of Joseph and Mary coming to Jerusalem, notwithstanding that Archelaus did still reign there, and leaving their substance and business for the service of God—that we should not allow vain excuses to hinder us from attending public worship.
   β. From the fact of Christ the Eternal Wisdom

deigning to listen humbly to these blind Pharisees and ignorant doctors—that we should not puff ourselves up with the consideration that we know better than those whom God has appointed over us as teachers, but in lowliness hearken to their instructions.

γ. From the fact of Mary, Joseph, and Jesus accomplishing the days, and not leaving before the feast was over—that we should not be eager to rush out of church in the middle of service, in the midst of the celebration of the Blessed Sacrament, before the completion of the sacrifice.

δ. From the fact of Mary and Joseph going to Jerusalem, "according to the custom of the feast,"—we learn to submit to all laudable customs, and not to set ourselves against them on the plea of our superior wisdom or understanding.

ε. From the fact of Mary and Jesus going to Jerusalem, whereas the law was not binding upon women and children—we learn not to rest satisfied with the letter, but to go on to the spirit; not to be content with mere conformity to the bare commandment of God, but with loving hearts to strive to "do more for His sake than of bounden duty is required." (The Church, for instance, bids us communicate three times in the year, but let us draw near oftener to the altar of God. The law of God requires us to give tithes of our goods, but let us give more, be liberal-hearted, and liberal-handed, and glad to distribute. S. B. G.)

ζ. From the fact of Christ being said to have increased in favour with God and man—let us learn to seek first the favour of God, and then the favour of good men will be added to us. Those who seek first the favour of men, often lose both that of man and God. Pilate, to find favour with Cæsar, fearing the accusation, "Thou art not Cæsar's friend," gave up Christ. And what did he gain? Nothing; he lost the favour of God and of Cæsar. By the one he was driven into exile, by the other he was cast down into hell.

Conclusion.

From like fearful end may Christ in His mercy keep us.

I will add a few specimens of the style of Matthias Faber. And I shall quote first some portions of an Easter sermon.

"See how our hope and confidence should be fixed on God. For the women went to the sepulchre through the morning twilight, without thought of the soldiers who guarded it, or of the sepulchral stone which closed it, for removing which they were far too weak. But as they drew nigh they considered this difficulty among themselves, saying, 'Who shall roll us away the stone from the door of the sepulchre?' And yet they turned not back despondingly, but resolutely persevered, trusting in God to provide the way and means.

And so it was as they trusted: by the providence of God the stone was removed by an angel, and at the sight of the angel the keepers fled in fear. Where human aid is wanting, there, if we trust in God, Divine aid is present."

"Behold the place, where we can see an image of the beatitude which we may expect on the Resurrection day. We see it in the angel. For he appeared as 'a young man,' and we all shall arise in 'the measure of the stature of the fulness of Christ,' in the flower of youth. His countenance was like lightning, and the bodies of the blessed shall be resplendent as the sun. He was vested in 'raiment white as snow,' signifying the glory and beatitude of the soul; 'And white robes were given unto every one of them' (Rev. vi. 11), those white robes which are promised to him that overcometh (Rev. iii. 5). He sat upon the stone—image of the constant and perpetual rest, ay, and regal dignity of the blessed in Heaven. And lastly, the angel was 'sitting on the right side,' for in Heaven there is nothing sinister and adverse, but all right, prosperous, and happy. But of this I have said enough elsewhere."

The following are from a Palm Sunday discourse:—

"Processions are in use in the Church on this day with palm-branches, in imitation of that in which Christ our Lord was this day conducted by the crowd and His disciples to the city of Jerusalem. But our Jerusalem is in Heaven, and thither are we advancing, led by Christ. With Him, and by Him, must we enter *the vision of peace* which Jerusalem signifies. In this procession he who takes not part, enters not Heaven.

For the idle and the spectators have no admission there. All those who took part in that triumphal entry into Jerusalem had something to do. Some loosed and led up the ass and colt, some laid their garments on them, some set Jesus thereon, some spread the public road with garments, some cut down branches from the trees, others again sang; the very beasts fulfilled their office, and bore their Creator. In like manner must we do something for Christ, if we would become partakers of His glory."

After having applied these several acts of the multitude to various conditions of life, in a practical manner, he comes to the seventh, "Others cried, saying, Hosanna to the Son of David," which he explains thus, "This do those who are happy and well-to-do in this present life, who are tossed by no storms of adversity, but sail on a tranquil sea. But there is danger in a life so calm in its state of wealth and pleasure. Yet they who have it, may also enter into the Blessed City, if they refer those good things which they enjoy to God, and diligently thank Him for them, 'singing and making melody in' their 'hearts to the Lord; giving thanks always for all things unto God and the Father in the name of our Lord Jesus Christ.' (Eph. v. 19, 20.) In like manner the state of felicity in which they were created was not injurious to the holy angels, for directly they were created they began to sing praises and give thanks to God for the benefit they had received, as God testified to Job, 'The morning stars sang together, and all the sons of God shouted for joy.' (Job xxxviii. 7.) And by reason of this praise, they were confirmed in a state of grace and felicity, and received glory. For this cause the holy patriarchs, though they abounded in earthly possessions, yet lost not their salvation. For indeed, they referred all their fortune, their prosperity, their abundance, to God. Thus Noah, saved from the deluge, 'builded an altar unto the Lord;' thus Abraham, having received a promise of the land for a possession, 'built an altar unto the Lord.' Thus did Isaac when he received the promise of the seed; thus did Jacob when delivered from the fear of Esau; thus, too, in acknowledgment of the good things they acquired, they called these things gifts of God; as Joseph called his sons, and as Jacob his sons and his flocks.

"If those who sail in prosperity, would but imitate these, and sing praises to God, they would reach the port of safety without difficulty."

I have said that Faber did not excel in simile. I must instance a few of his attempts at illustration of this nature, to corroborate my statement.

In one sermon, already quoted, he speaks of persons who begin repentance, and then soon break off from their pious exercises, to return to their old state of torpor and indifference, and he says they resemble frogs, which crawl a little way out of their swamp, but, at the least sound to alarm them, flop into their slough again.

In another sermon, Faber rebukes those who ask thoughtlessly in prayer, and make no use of the blessings given them in answer, and he tells them they are like the boys who on bonfire night go about begging wood with the song,—

"Lieber Herz Sanct Veith,
Bescher uns ein Scheitt."

"O dear Saint Vitus,
Grant us a faggot!"

And what use do they make of the faggot when they have it? asks the preacher. Why they make a fire with it, on which they may jump, till they have stamped it out!

And in speaking of the obedience of servants to their masters, he says it should resemble that of the man who is being shaved. Such a man turns his head this way, or that way, puts his chin up, or puts it down, in obedience to the slightest gesture and sign of the barber.

Faber is fond of quoting popular sayings and proverbs; some of which I give in his quaint old German :—

1. Wer sich mischt unter die Klew,
   Dem fressen die Saw.
2. Ein guter Zoll
   Ist spardir woll.
3. Wo tein gleicher Glauben ist
   Da auch tein Recht, betrawen ist.
4. Sanct Catyarein,
   Schliest die Thur ein.

This is in reference to St. Katharine's day closing the door of the Christian year.

I must find space for one story related by Faber on New Year's Day.

A farmer once told a wise man that he was daily becoming poorer; whereupon he received from the wise man a casket, with the advice to take it daily into his kitchen, his garden, his storehouse, his vineyard, his cellar, his stable, and his field; and then, on the condition that the box was not opened till the year's end, the sage promised wealth to the farmer. The husbandman obeyed implicitly: in the kitchen he found the cook wasting the meat, in the cellar the vats leaking, in the fields the labourers idling, in the garden the vegetables unhoed. All these disorders were rectified, and by the year's end the man's fortune was doubled. Then he opened the casket, and found in it a slip of paper, on which was written:—

> "Wills du Dag dir reichlich geling
> Solves taglich zu deinem Ding."

Which, Faber adds, is like the German saying, The best soil for a field is that in the farmer's shoe.

# PHILIP VON HARTUNG.

This very popular preacher was born on the 25th October, 1629, at Theising, in Bohemia. He entered the novitiate of the Jesuit order in 1645, at the age of sixteen. He spent his early life in different colleges, but finally he ascertained that his vocation was to be a preacher, and thenceforth he devoted his time and energies to the composition of sermons. He preached most frequently at Sternberg, in Moravia, and at Glogau, in Silesia. He died at Eger on the 9th March, 1682, aged fifty-three. The greater part of his works were published after his decease.

1. R. P. Philippi Hartung, Concio tergemina rustica, civica, aulica, in Dominicas; Colon., 1680, 4to., 2 vols.; Egræ, 1686, fol.; Colon., 1709, 4to.; Norimbergæ, 1718, fol. Conciones tergeminæ in Festa; Norimbergæ, 1711, 4to. Ibid., 1718, fol., 2 vols.

2. Philippicæ sive Invectivæ LX. in Notorios Peccatores. Pro singulis totius anni Dominicis. Ægræ, 1687, fol.; Calissii, 1688, 4to.; Augustæ et Dilingæ, 1695, 4to.

3. Problemata Evangelica; Egræ, 1689, fol.; Augustæ et Dilingæ, 1695, 4to.

4. Heiliger Tag; Prag, 1733, 12mo. Heiliger Tag und gute Nacht; Rauffbeyern, 1745, 12mo.

The sermons of Philip von Hartung are very unequal; some of them are polished gems, others are very rough diamonds; but none are without value. The preacher had his mind stored with matter, but he was wanting in the art of nicely digesting it, and reproducing what fermented in his brain, in a pleasant form. At least, so we must judge of him from his published Latin sermons; but it is quite open to question whether these discourses were delivered as they are written. I am rather inclined to regard them as his schemes from which he preached, the outlines which he developed extempore. And this I think the more probable, as the vast majority are short. It must be remembered that only one edition of the sermons appeared during the author's lifetime, and that, only two years before his death. In this edition are contained the Sunday sermons, but not those for the festivals.

Hartung gives at least three sermons for each Sunday and festival: one addressed to a rural congregation, the second to a town audience, and the third delivered before Court. As might be expected, the *concio aulica* is the poorest of the set, the preacher being less at his ease, and more fettered by conventionalities. The rustic sermons are capital. He preaches on broad facts of religion, Sunday after Sunday, with striking vigour, considerable beauty, and no small amount of originality.

During the Sundays in Advent he preaches to the rural congregation on the Last Judgment. The first sermon is on the appearance in Heaven of the cross, the sign of the Son of Man; the second is on the trumpet-call waking the dead; the third on the examination of the risen ones; the fourth on the final dooms of good and bad; each of these is a most striking sermon.

From the first Sunday after the Epiphany to Quinquagesima, Hartung preaches on Hell: the absence of Jesus, its chief woe, the hunger and thirst of the damned, the gloom, the tears, the horror of the abode, the undying worm of conscience, the fire, the eternity of the punishment, the murmurs of the damned, &c.

From the first Sunday in Lent to Palm Sunday he preaches on Death: the time of death the season of temptation, the time of death the moment of transfiguration, the time of death the time for confession and communion, the time of death the moment of supreme joy, &c.

At the same time he has another series of rural sermons from Septuagesima to the close of Lent, on our Lord's Passion.

From Easter Day, Hartung preaches upon Heaven: the beauty of the glorified body fills three discourses; he speaks then of the harmony of Heaven, the immutability of the joy, the vastness and beauty of the abode of the redeemed, the delight of the five senses in Heaven, and the thoughts of Heaven.

Throughout Trinity, Hartung preaches upon God. I shall give two sermons of the preacher, the one on Hell, the other on Heaven.

First Sunday after the Epiphany.
Rural Sermon.
On Hell.—I.
The absence of Jesus, the chief woe of the lost.

Luke ii. 48. *Thy father and I have sought thee sorrowing.*

1. He loses much who in a moment loses his wealth, as did Job.

He loses more who loses the favour of a king, and the love of an intimate friend, as did Absalom.

He loses more yet who loses himself, as did Ahithophel.

But he loses most who loses Jesus; for he who loses Jesus loses every thing, a treasure above price, the best of friends, the surest of counsellors, his *all in all*.

"Omnia si perdas, Jesum servare memento,
Ipse tibi Jesus *omnia solus* erit."

The names Jesus and Jehovah are very similar, as St. Jerome observes, for what Jehovah *signifies*, that Jesus *is*—all in all. Oh! how sweetly does Ambrose exclaim, "Christ is our all."

Art thou an infant? He is thy mother, her breast, her milk.

Art thou aged? He is thy staff, thy stay.

Art thou a boy? He is thy path, thy way.

Art thou sick? He is thy physician and thy medicine.

Art thou dying? He buries thy soul, not in the bosom of Abraham, but in His own pierced side, and thy body He lays in the field which He purchased for thee at the price of His blood, the field of the Church, His Bride.

Christ is all to us. He who loses Him, loses all. Truly, if Micah could say when his idols were removed, *Ye have taken away my gods which I made,—and what have I more?* (Judg. xviii. 24;) far more truly may he complain who sees himself deprived of Jesus.

And this will be the chief woe of the damned—that Jesus is irrevocably lost to them. For if He were in hell, it would be no hell, as Heaven without Him would be no Heaven, as the Royal Psalmist exclaims: *Whom have I in Heaven but Thee?* To be with Jesus, is to be in Paradise, as the poor thief learned, when he was assured that he should be with Jesus, and therefore be in Paradise: *To-day shalt thou be with Me in Paradise.*

To be away from Jesus is to be in hell. Wherefore the sentence of the Judge is: *Depart from Me, ye cursed.* To be separated from Jesus, and that for ever; ah! that is *the* malediction of all, that a hell deeper than hell itself.

But how is it that we esteem this loss at so small a price? that we lose Jesus knowingly, wilfully, for a momentary pleasure, for a point of honour, for a nothing at all; and having lost Him, seek Him not sorrowing?

Our own gross ignorance is the cause, readily consenting to sin, and so losing us the dear presence of Jesus.

\* \* \* \* \* \*

2. How great this loss is, and how great a grief arises from this loss, those who have experienced the loss know.

Mary Magdalene saw her beloved Jesus fall seven times beneath the great weight of the cross, she beheld Him hang for three hours upon the cross, she saw Him taken down from the tree and laid in a sepulchre, and yet not one Evangelist says that she shed a single tear. But on the most festive day of the Resurrection, when the angels sang their paschal hallelujah in full choir, when mourning was laid aside for garments white and clean, when the dead themselves rose for joy from their graves, and the dawn blushed a fairer pink than heretofore, and the sun, rejoicing *as a giant to run his course*, scattered brighter than wonted beams, THEN Magdalene wept inconsolably, nor deigned to look at the angels who asked, *Woman, why weepest thou? for*, says the Evangelist, she had *bowed down* her face to the earth, as though beaten down and crushed beneath the burden of her sorrow.

But why this strange paradox! that she should not weep at the time for tears, and now not laugh at the time for laughter? Magdalene's answer explains all: *They have taken away my Lord.* This was her sole and worthy cause of tears—the absence of her Lord. "She wept more," says Augustine, "because He was removed from the sepulchre, than because He was slain upon the tree." When He was on the cross, she stood by; when He was entombed, she sat over against the sepulchre; dying she was near Him, risen she was parted from Him—therefore flowed her tears. Truly may St. Ber-

G

nard say: "So sweet is Jesus to all who taste of Him, so beautiful to all who behold Him, so dear to all who embrace Him, that a little moment of absence is greatest cause of sorrow." But oh! what will it then be, to lose Him for ever and ever!

3. To this example of a female disciple who loved much, let us add that of a male disciple who loved very much, that from both we may learn what it is to lose Jesus. Peter, inseparable, as it were, from Christ, according to his own testimony, *Lord, to whom shall we go? Thou hast the words of eternal life*,—Peter, I say, when he saw his Master rise from the supper of the law, and gird Himself with the towel, pour water into a basin, and stoop to wash his feet, refused to permit Him to do it: *Thou shalt never wash my feet.* Oh, Peter! hast thou forgotten thy words to thy Lord: *Bid me come to Thee on the water?* And why wilt thou not dip thy feet in water when thy Lord cometh to thee? Thou art ready to go with Him *to prison and to death*, and that thou mayest go the better, He who giveth *His angels charge concerning thee*, is conforming thy feet that they may bear thee up, *lest thou dash thy foot against a stone.* Ay! He is placing His hands beneath thy feet to bear thee up Himself, lest thou stumble at the stone of stumbling and rock of offence. Why delay? Why shrink back? Why recoil? God loveth not headstrong piety, nor an obstinate self-will! Listen, Peter, to what Christ answers thee: *If I wash thee not, thou hast no part with Me.* So many words, so many lightnings! by these Peter is threatened, not with prison and darkness, not with horrors and

wretchedness, not with pyres and wheels, but with the absence of Christ Himself, *Thou hast no part with Me.* . . . Touched by this lightning-stroke, Peter exclaims: *Lord, not my feet only, but also my hands and my head.*

4. . . . . .

5. Fatal will be that last sentence: *Depart from Me, ye cursed, into everlasting fire.* Here observe that the first portion of the sentence refers to expulsion from Christ's presence as the chief pain of hell. Of which says St. Chrysostom: "This pain is worse than to be tortured in the flames." And St. Bruno: "Let torments be added to torments, let cruel ministers cruelly rack, let all kinds of scourges increase their severity, but let us not be deprived of God, whose absence would be the worst of tortures." And that this may be confirmed by the mouths of three witnesses, B. Laurentius Justiniani says, "The interminable want of the beatific vision will excel all other woes."

Certainly the damned would feel no pain if they could see Jesus. Three children were cast into the burning fiery furnace of Babylon, and they trampled on the flames, they sang among their torments, and called upon all creatures to unite with them in praise. Would you know the reason? We have it from the mouth of the hostile king: *Lo! I see four men loose, walking in the midst of the fire, and they have no hurt; and the form of the fourth is like the Son of God.* The form, the very image only, of the Son of God was sufficient to remove all power from the fierce element, to turn torment into jubilee, punishment into delight, a furnace into a joke (*focum in jocum;* a pun), a torturer's pyre into festive flames. No less would the damned rejoice if they could thus behold the Son of God, and would set at nought fire, hell, and damnation.

6. Oh! if after myriads of years they were given a chance of obtaining one thing from Christ, would they ask of Him any thing else but that which the blind man required—*Lord, that I may see?* Why did the damned Dives ask that Lazarus might come with a drop of water at the tip of his finger to cool his parched tongue? Why did he not rather demand a refreshing shower, or a pleasant rill of cool water to flow into his throat? It was because he desired the presence of the glorified Lazarus. By that presence all his pains would be relieved, his hell would be turned into Paradise. The longed-for Lazarus is the very Son of God, who suffered poverty at the gate of the rich, asking for a little crumb of comfort, but in vain; rejected by the Jews, the dogs of Gentiles came, and found healing in His wounds.

Now the damned desire of the Father that He should send His Son, who with the finger of God's right hand, the Holy Spirit, might touch the stream of celestial joys, and let one drop distil into the consuming fire, to refresh the lost for one moment, to give them for one instant a glimpse of the beauty of that radiant countenance. But in vain; in vain they ask, they cry, they weep; they shall see the face of Jesus no more.

The sentence was pronounced against the children of outer darkness when God said, *My face will I turn also from them.* The hiding of that countenance is the source of all ills. *My face will I turn from them!* they have set the face of men before them in the place of Mine. They have loved the beauty of human countenances rather than the glory of Mine which is divine. *My face will I turn from them!* I, who turned not My face from those who spat upon it, and buffeted Me. *My face will I turn from them,* and My face is *as the sun, and they shall never see light;* My face, which is the source of all gladness; *Lord, lift Thou up the light of Thy countenance upon us. Thou hast put gladness in my heart,* and they shall be sad; My face, the prospect of beholding which tempers more than did the hopes of possessing Rachel. They shall labour for ever without rest, or solace, or refreshment. And this is the sum of their woes, that Jesus, whom they lost in the way of life, they find not again, and shall not see or grasp through ages evermore.

7. Oh, weeping mother of Jesus! who soughtest Him whom thou hadst lost, through no fault of thine own; by that pain, that anxiety, that aching void thou didst endure through three days when thy Son was absent; keep, I pray thee, thy Jesus and my Jesus in our souls, that we may never lose Him through our grave offence. Rather may the world perish, and all the vanity therein, than that thy Jesus should be lost to us! Rather may health and life, and good report, and fortune, hope and all things perish, if only we may keep Jesus, without whom all things else are nought, for He is all in all.

## The Second Sunday after Easter.

### Rural Sermon.

#### *On Heaven.*—VI.

The unity and concord of the Heaven-dwellers.

John x. 16. *There shall be one fold and one shepherd.*

1. And when will that happy time at last arrive, when the fold will be but one, and one the Shepherd, so that once more all shall be *of one heart and of one soul* among those that believe?

Alas! the fold of Christ has ever been broken through: Nicolaitans and Corinthians in apostolic times, then Gnostics, Manichæans, Arians, Donatists. These were followed by Iconoclasts, Albigenses, Hussites and sects of this age, which I will not name [1].

Shall there ever be discord in the faith? Shall we in the same fold be ever severed in heart? . . . Unity is not to be found here: not here, but in Heaven, where the Pastor is one, and the God triune; where the flock is twofold, human and angelic. Of the concord of the blessed shall I now speak. . . .

2. There is not so great a variety among garden flowers or meadow herbs, among forest trees, among fishes of the sea or birds of the air, among meats at a feast or nations upon earth, as there is among the saints. Yet, though so great is the variety, great also is the harmony. The Psalmist, considering the won-

---

[1] Notice the gentle and loving spirit of the Jesuit here; he avoids giving offence without retiring from his position.

drous unity of the saints, breaks forth into praise to God, who *maketh men to be of one mind in an house.* They have the same will, not as brothers, but as one man, and yet they are of all tribes, and tongues, and nations, and they are a *great multitude which no man can number,* yet all understand each other, for each can speak all tongues.

The variety of nations, and sexes, and states, and merits, and natures will afford delight. The angels in their three hierarchies, in each of which are three choirs, and in each choir nine mansions; thus are they divided, yet in this great crowd there is no crowding. The limbs are not bound to the body as closely as the elect are united in the bonds of their charity. Why are the members of the body so united? Because, forsooth, they communicate into one spirit. Though their natures may differ, and their offices vary, one soul conciliates them; then how much more will the Divine Spirit, by whom all the elect live, make unity such as this and much more excellent. None will contradict, none contend with, none emulate, none envy another. *Without are dogs.* In that country there will be no Cain to slay his brother Abel; in that family there will be no Jacob to hate Esau; in that house no Ishmael to contend with Isaac; in that kingdom no Saul to persecute David; in that college no Judas to betray his Master. Hence their exceeding joy. *Behold, how good and joyful a thing it is, brethren, to dwell together in unity!* All will the same thing, for all have but one rule which they observe, the will of God, against which they can rebel no more. . . . . . Wherefore, because it is the will of

God that Peter should be greater than James, each will be content, each will rejoice in the joy of the other as though it were his own. Consequently, St. Augustine says, "Each will be glad in the beatitude of another, as much as in his own ineffable joy, and he who has friends has as many joys. Whatever is needful, whatever pleases, is there; all riches, all rest, all solace. For what can be wanting to him where God is, to whom nothing lacks? There, all know God without error, see Him without end, praise Him without fatigue, love Him without fail. And in this delight, all repose full of God; cleaving ever to blessedness, they are blessed; contemplating ever eternity, they are eternal." See how good and how pleasant! so pleasant, that one day granted in Heaven in the enjoyment of the society of the blessed would be of sufficient value to make us resign all the delights of this life, to make us renounce all evil companionship. *One day in Thy courts is better than a thousand.* For all joys, all pleasures of this world, as compared to the perennial delight in Heaven flowing from the vision of God and the society of the saints, are but as a drop to the ocean.

3. Man is a social animal, and though he may abound in all, yet if he have not a companion he is not happy. Let a man be shut up in a palace or a garden, and be left alone, he will soon weary of the solitude, and ask to be either let go or to have a companion admitted. God Himself judged this when He saw that it was not well for Adam to be alone, even in Paradise. Seneca said divinely, "The possession of no good is pleasant without a companion."

God, though He needs none, yet seems to affect society, for He says, *My delights were with the sons of men.* Indeed, when He designed to form man, He said, *Let us make man in our image, after our likeness. Let us make,* one labour of the Three Persons; and the one work is social man. *After our likeness,* that as there is plurality of Persons in one Nature, so there might be a plurality of bodies, yet a unity of souls. But this unity will not be perfect, this likeness complete, except in the celestial Paradise, where, says St. John, *we shall be like Him;* then, indeed, many will be one, and one like all, in the admirable unity of souls. Drexelius ingeniously observes, "God found an admirable art, by which a happy one might make the joys of many myriads his own, and thus each might be hundredfold happy." The art consists in this, that the thought is deep rooted in each of the blessed ones, a thought sweeter than honey: God loves me intimately and infinitely, and I love God with my whole being; and these all love me, and I love them; eternally shall I be loved, eternally loving. Hence the immense joy which each feels in the other's happiness. . . . Isaiah beholding this celestial charity, this goodly unity in the land flowing with milk and honey, says, *My people shall dwell in a peaceable habitation, and in sure dwellings, and in quiet resting-places.*

*Shall sit down* (Vulg.). This the position, this the mark of perennial rest. Now we stand and fight till we drop into our graves. . . . *In the beauty of peace* (Vulg.). Beautiful is that which is perfect; in Heaven peace is most beautiful, for there is it altogether most perfect. *In the tabernacles of confidence* (Vulg.). When six hundred thousand men went forth out of Egypt, they dwelt in tabernacles, but not in confidence; in tabernacles of fear and anxiety, for the way before them was to be opened by the sword, and the foe was to be dreaded on every side. But in Heaven there is no foe, nothing hostile, no ambushes, no heartburnings; but security and confidence, unity and charity; therefore they sit down in *wealthy rest* (Vulg.), for they will not only possess what they have hoped for, but more than they hoped for, ay! more than they were capable of hoping for. One possesses what all possess, and therefore they are all of *one heart and of one soul*.

4. But how will it be, that with such disparity of rewards, there will be no strife and envy? This may best be explained by a simile. If a father had ten sons of different statures, and were to dress them each alike in silk, the smallest would not envy the greatest because his breast was wider, his sleeves fuller, his cloak longer, but would be content with his own little tunic, and would be unwilling to exchange it. So, too, the eldest would be well pleased in the little brother because he was suitably equipped. The same too in a banquet, where each may drink what, and how much, he likes. But St. Augustine has a more graceful simile, taken from the strings of a harp. The strings are of various lengths, but when struck they produce harmony. "The saints will have their own harmonious differences in degrees, just as the sweetest

music is that produced by diverse, but not adverse sounds."

5. He who would attain to this most blessed society, ought to be in the fold of Christ, that one, true, good Church Catholic, which is the fold of Christ, beyond which is neither unity of doctrine nor the bond of the Good Shepherd's charity.

Secondly, let the Christians who are in this fold learn from the sheep to seek unity. Let them remain closely bound to each other, and not bite each other as dogs, nor rend as wolves, nor kick as horses, nor butt as goats; so, O Christian, abstain from tossing thy neighbour on the horns of pride, injuring him with the bark of envy, rending him with the tooth of detraction; but like a gentle lamb cleave to the Good Shepherd, and thou shalt be of the dear sheep of Christ. For what St. Bonaventura says seraphically, touching the religious state, is to be repeated a thousand times: "There is no greater proof of a man's predestination, and that he is conforming himself to God, than that he should exhibit himself to be gentle and patient," and I add, that he should show his love for concord and unity.

I think that no one can peruse these two sermons, which I have given almost entire, curtailing them but slightly, without being convinced of the overflowing charity and deep-seated piety of the holy man who wrote them. Whatever there may be of crudity in the style, every thought gushes from the pure spring of the love of God, open and flowing in the heart of the good

Jesuit. *He that believeth on Me, out of his belly shall flow rivers of living water,* may justly be applied to Philip von Hartung. Many and many a rill of the water of Life may be lighted on in the garden of delights contained in his volumes. Often, perhaps, the water is discoloured, but more often is it limpid and crystalline as when it leaped out of the fount of God.

In style Hartung resembles the more earnest preachers of dissent, because he speaks from the heart. *Out of the abundance of the heart the mouth speaketh.* If our preachers had the zeal and the love of God which was found among the great Catholic orators, and is still to be discovered among dissenting ministers, there would be fewer complaints of the barrenness of the land, less deadness to the calls of God in professed Church-goers. It is quite impossible for a preacher to effect the slightest good unless he feels what he says from the depths of his soul; it is hopeless for him to expect to draw hearts to the love of Jesus, if he knows not what that love is. And the sermon, however eloquent and finished in style, will never convert sinners, unless its inspiration is derived from God; and that inspiration can alone be obtained by prayer.

He who prays much is filled with a power of winning souls quite inexplicable; he sheds a sort of magnetic influence upon hearts, drawing them to Christ; and, though the words be few and ill-chosen, they can do a work for God which the most polished masterpiece of elocution would be powerless to effect.

I think the story is told of Francis Borgia, that he was asked to preach at a certain church in a distant city. On his arrival he was too ill to speak, and he requested some one to occupy his place. "No!" said the priest who had summoned him; "only mount the pulpit, say nothing, and come away." He did so; hearts were touched, people burst into tears, and the confessionals were filled with penitents. He was a man of *Prayer*.

# JOSEPH DE BARZIA.

I know of no preacher of his age who comes so near to Paolo Segneri, the great luminary of Italian eloquence, as this Spaniard, De Barzia. He flourished at the beginning of the seventeenth century, and was Bishop of Cadiz.

His works are :—

Christianus animarum excitator. Auctore J. de Barzia, Soc. Jesu; Augustæ Vindelicorum, 1721, 2 vols. folio.

There is, I believe, a mistake in this title; Joseph de Barzia was not a Jesuit; at all events, the brothers Bächer have not included him in their catalogue.

Compendium excitatoris Christiani; lingua primum Hispanica vulgatum ipsomet ab Auctore Rdo. D. Josepho de Barzia Episcopo Gaditano, nunc demum Latine versum a R. P. Petro Gummersbach, Soc. Jesu; Coloniæ, 1724, 4to.

Manductio ad excitationem Christianorum; seu, Sermones Missionales. Auctore Jos. de Barzia; Augustæ Vindelic., 1732, 2 vols. in one, 8vo. Ibid. 1737, 2 vols. in one, 8vo.

The sermons of De Barzia are model mission-discourses; they are interesting, pointed, full of illustration and anecdote, and are eminently qualified to arrest the attention, and arouse the consciences of the hearers.

The good Bishop possessed the art of never suffering the attention of his audience to flag. He carefully avoided wearing his subject thread-bare, and the moment he saw that his shot had taken effect, he opened a new battery from another point altogether, yet aimed at the same object.

His knowledge of the Bible is wonderful, even for a Roman Catholic Post-Mediæval preacher; his sermons teem with Scriptural illustrations of the most apposite character, culled from every portion of Holy Writ. It is not that he affects quotations from Scripture in the manner of Helmesius, who, in an Advent sermon, could make one hundred and seventy-five quotations, but that he found in his Bible an inexhaustible store of illustration for every subject which he handled.

The majority of Mediæval sacred orators, and their immediate followers, seemed to think, and consequently speak, in Scripture terms, but De Barzia preaches to unlettered men, who knew little or nothing of their Bibles, beyond the broad outlines of sacred history, and who would not recognize quotations from the prophetic books or the Epistles. He therefore avoids these to a considerable extent, unless he can point them out severally as words of Scripture, and confines himself chiefly to the narrative portions of the inspired volume. He selects an incident which can bear upon his subject, relates it in the most vigorous style, and then applies it with force and effect.

And these happy selections show such thorough acquaintance with the sacred writings, that it is impossible not to see that Holy Scripture formed the staple of the good Bishop's meditations, night and day. His sermons are eminently practical; they are not dogmatic. De Barzia makes no attempt to instruct in Catholic doctrine, he presupposes that his hearers are orthodox, he does not suggest the possibility of there being a heretic among them, he makes no attempt to arm them for the conflict of the faith, but he goes straight as an arrow to their consciences, and stirs them to the perception of their moral obligations.

In this he differs widely from the German and French preachers of his age, who seldom preached without firing a broadside at heresy, and generally took the opportunity to furnish their hearers with arguments in favour of Catholic doctrines and practices.

De Barzia is more subjective than the other preachers of his day, and he excels in sermons calculated to strike terror into the impenitent heart. Each man has his special line, and his was the declaration of God's judgments. Marchantius would melt the stony heart with love, De Barzia shatter it with fear. And yet his soul was full of tenderness and the love of God, which exude from him occasionally, as the aromatic gum from the frankincense.

For instance, take the following:—" Ungrateful sinner, let me speak to thee in the name of Jesus crucified—'Why!' says He to thee, 'who filled thee with such rage against Me? *What iniquity have your fathers found in Me?* (Jer. ii. 5.) Of what sin canst thou charge Me, that thou ragest so furiously against Me?

*Many good things have I showed you;* I have displayed abundant charity, I have poured forth many benefits; *for which of those works do ye stone Me?* (John x. 32.) Art thou enraged against Me because I brought thee into existence out of nothing? Art thou vexed because I have watchfully preserved thee? because I have brought thee to a saving faith? Dost thou count it an injury that I gave up life and honour, blood and all, upon the cross for thee? . . . . Come now, answer thou Me, wherefore art thou enraged against Me?' O Jesu, best beloved! cease to inquire! I own that there is no cause, I acknowledge my audacity, and I bewail it! Flow, my tears, flow, and streaming over my cheeks, testify to my sorrow! Break, O heart, break, through excess of love! I acknowledge, I own, I see clearly my condition. What have I done! I have returned Thee evil for good, and hatred for Thy good will. Which was it, love or enmity, which crucified Thee? O Lord! it was love, and it was enmity. Thine the love, mine the enmity."

The following abstract is a good specimen of the Bishop's quaintness.

The Seventeenth Sunday after Pentecost.

Sermon III.

God is to be loved with the whole heart, and even light sins are to be avoided.

Matt. xxii. 37. *Thou shalt love the Lord thy God with all thy heart.*

The unhappy Ishbosheth, son of Saul, was slain in

his own house, after the destruction of his father's army. How, think you? Was the door open for the foe to enter? It was open: for he had been winnowing wheat; and they *came about the heat of the day to the house of Ishbosheth, who lay on a bed at noon. And they came thither into the midst of the house, as though they would have fetched wheat; and they smote him.* (2 Sam. iv. 5, 6.) Here was neglect of ordinary watchfulness, a little heedlessness, a little drowsiness, a little care for the wheat, leading to loss of life. St. Eucher says truly, "When man loses the solicitude of discretion, he leaves the door open for the ingress of evil spirits to the slaying of his soul."

Truly, many an ill has come to us through this indifference to our danger, through carelessness for our spiritual peril.

Oh, what precious swords are rusted, because they are not drawn from their scabbards!

Oh, what noble horses become sluggish in their stalls, because they are not exercised!

Oh, what crystalline pools nourish reptiles, because they are not stirred!

Oh, what great souls, living in honour and purity, have fallen into an abyss of sin, because they have been negligent! "For," says Lessius, "he who serves God negligently, deserves in return that God should not exert Himself to care so greatly for him."

Little venial faults begin to accumulate and increase till the whole moral nature is clouded by them. The intellect is darkened, the fervour of charity cooled, the spirit stained; the strength fails in temptation, the soul is enervated in prayer, the whole man is neglectful in the practice of good works; and why? Because he has neglected to purge himself of his little faults, to struggle against his infirmities. King David often cried to God, *Incline Thine ear unto me ; bow down Thine ear to me.* (Ps. xvii. 6 ; xxxi. 2 ; lxxi. 2.) It was not enough that God should hear his prayer, but He must also bow down over him. Just as sick men, when their voices are broken and faint with disease, require the physician to incline his ear to their lips; so does David, well knowing how weakened and broken is his prayer through venial sins and daily transgressions, ask God in like manner to incline His ear to him.

Oh, how great is the evil arising from little ills! A grain of sand, how light it is! but many grains accumulated will sink a stately vessel! How light is a drop of rain! yet many gathered into one stream will submerge houses! How trifling is the loss of a little tile! yet it will admit the rain to rot the timber, to break down the walls, and to produce a ruin!

In like manner one little venial sin may lead to destruction, if it be neglected. It is a trifle looked at by itself, but it has brought a soul to perdition, in that, as St. Thomas asserts, a venial sin may dispose towards the commission of a deadly sin!

It is worth noting, the manner in which the sea-crab gets an oyster and eats it. In the morning early the oyster gapes, that it may bask in the sunbeams. Then up steals the crab, not boldly advancing upon the fish, or it would at once close its shell and escape him, or clutch him tight by his claws. What course does the crafty animal adopt? It takes a little pebble and tosses it into the oyster. This prevents the valves from closing, and then he rushes up and devours the oyster at his leisure.

Soul of man! just so comes the evil one towards thee; not alluring thee to some sin of horrible deadliness, but flinging a little pebble—a tiny fault—into thy heart, and if thou cast it not from thee at once, but keepest thy heart still unclosed, he obtaineth an entry and destroyeth thee utterly.

Take another specimen. The following passages are condensed from a sermon on the vanity of all the labour of sinners, and the lamentations of lost souls when they behold in retrospect their life squandered in empty trifles.

### The Fourth Sunday after Pentecost.

### Sermon III.

Luke v. 5. *We have toiled all the night, and have taken nothing.*

Those words of Job are worthy of notice, *I have made my bed in the darkness.* I will explain them to you by the use of a simile.

A lighted candle is given to a servant that he may retire to rest by its light, after that he has made his bed. The fellow snatches up the candle and begins to wander about the house, dawdling over this or that, gossiping with one or another, till the candle is expended, flickers up, and dies out. Then, in hurry, he runs to his chamber, but he is without light, and he is constrained to make and to retire to his *bed in the dark-*

ness. O Christian soul! if you sigh for the rest of eternal glory, know that God has given to you for the very purpose of finding it, and preparing for it, the taper of life. If you consume that life in idleness and in vanities, you will have to make your bed in the darkness, and in the outer darkness lie down to rest,—to rest! oh, no! to seek rest, and find none on that ill-made couch, to toil all the night of eternity and to take nothing; for the time of preparation has been wasted, and the work which was to be done has been neglected till the allotted time for doing it has expired.

Of the virtuous woman declared King Solomon, *She layeth her hands to the spindle.* Where is the flax? "Spun," says St. Ambrose. See what a mystery is involved here! The flax is attached to the head of the distaff, and the spun thread is twisted round the spindle. "On the distaff is that which is to be done, on the spindle that which is done," says the same Father. Therefore does Solomon commend the just soul which has accomplished its work, not that which has its work to accomplish: for that soul which has finished its work is secure, not that which has to commence it. Look, then, to thy spindle, see if of the work God has set before thee any is spun off and completed; if so, there lay thy hand, for there is thy virtue, there thy security. Christian man! that the praise of the virtuous soul may be thine, it behoveth thee not to have a handful of flax at thy distaff-head, but a full spindle at thy side: not purposes, but acts; not confession to be made, but confession made; not restitution to be accomplished, but restitution accomplished;

not injuries to be forgiven, but injuries already forgiven. Things that are future are but flax on the distaff-head, flax which will blaze up and leave no trace; but things of the present are thread spun, and therefore is the virtuous woman commended, who layeth her hands to the spindle.

Terrible is the sentence of God in Deuteronomy: *If I whet My glittering sword, and Mine hand take hold of judgment; I will render vengeance to Mine enemies.* (Deut. xxxii. 41.) And where will God whet His glittering sword? Where are blades usually whetted? Let us look. Surely on a whirling circular stone. And on what stone will God whet His sword? I reply, on that stony heart of the sinner, which is ever revolving, never at rest. Watch the grindstone a little while. See how it plunges down into a trough of turbid, foul, and muddy water. O stone, stone! why rush down into this filth? Rise up, rise up from this uncleanness. I put my hand to it, I set the stone in motion. How easily is it made to revolve! It moves—it leaves that sink of filth—it mounts upwards. In vain! It whirls round, and with a rush seeks again its bed of pollution.

Heart of sinner, hard and stony! why dost thou not emerge from the corruption in which thou wallowest? 'I will emerge,' thou repliest. Why dost thou not leave thy enmities, thy passions, thy shameful uncleanness? 'I will leave them,' is thy answer. And yet nothing comes of these fine promises. Always on the move like the grindstone, you never remove from the trough of slime; always leaving sin, that with fresh relish you may plunge into it again.

Know, you sinners who are so full of good resolutions which come to nought, so full of promises of amendment which end in relapse, that it is on whirling grindstones such as you that *the glittering sword* of Divine vengeance is whetted. *If I whet My glittering sword, . . . I will render vengeance to Mine enemies.*

To whom, I ask, will He render vengeance? To His enemies; to those such as you who have such excellent purposes, but who have never accomplished one good purpose. Then when that sword is whetted, too late will you exclaim with the lost, 'We have erred, we have erred, we have taken nothing!' Wretched sinners! do you hear these threats, these warnings, these words of God calling you to repentance? You hear, and yet you stop your ears as the deaf adder; you despise, you laugh, you mock, you harden into stone!

Well, then, be hard as stone, have your laugh out, despise as you will, stop your ears! you are at liberty so to do! Yet, mark me, the time will assuredly come when the laugh will be turned against you.

*Because I have called, and ye refused; I have stretched out My hand, and no man regarded; but ye have set at nought all My counsel, and would none of My reproof:* awful is that which follows! *I also will laugh at your calamity; I will mock when your fear cometh.* (Prov. i. 24—26.) O good God! O goodness immeasurable, dost Thou laugh at the destruction of Thy sons! Alas! terrible laughter is that indeed.

Hannibal is said, after the subjection of Carthage by Rome, to have walked through the city, and, as he saw the tears and heard the wailing of the people who groaned under the terrible burden imposed upon them by the conquerors, to have laughed. Then, when his fellow-citizens rose up against him in indignation, he replied, " I laugh not from joy to see your bondage; but I laugh at your tears, now too late, now in vain; for had you in proper time fought as men, now you would not be weeping as women."

Behold, O sinners, as in a picture, your tears and God's laughter : you bewailing your misery, and God laughing at your tears : you sobbing through eternity under the burden of the Devil's rule, and God laughing at your sobs: you lamenting in the agony of eternal fire, and God laughing at your lamentations: and all— because when as Christians you might have fought the good fight, now, when too late, you break forth into tears which are vain, and into lamentations which are fruitless.

Surely this is a very terrible, yet striking sermon, one sure to tell on rude and uncultivated minds, from the vigour of the moral application, and the richness of the imagery.

There are some very remarkable passages in the next sermon, which is on the subject of the merit of good works consisting in the inward disposition, and not in the magnitude of the outward act.

De Barzia relates the story of the anointing of David. He pictures Samuel before the sons of Jesse admiring the stalwart form of Eliab, and the stature of Aminadab, and thinking that one of these must be the destined king. Yet no—it is none of these. The word of God bids him anoint David, the youngest, the feeblest, the shepherd boy: for *the Lord said unto Samuel, Look not on his countenance. ... Man looketh on the outward appearance, but the Lord looketh on the heart.* Oh! exclaims the Bishop, how different are the judgments of God from those of man!

Men often preach up some act as great and wonderful which is worthless in God's judgment. Men estimate the quality of a work from the outside, God weighs the inward intent of the soul: as says the wisest of kings: *All the ways of a man are clean in his own eyes; but the Lord weigheth the spirits.* (Prov. xvi. 2.) This is the difference between the judgments of God and of man, and this difference will be made manifest when all things shall be revealed before the Divine tribunal. To that judgment-seat will come the Christian soul and there give account of all its works, its alms, its fasts, its prayers: boastfully perhaps it will advance, resting on the multitude of these, reckoning to enter through them into life everlasting, and to merit the crown of immortality.

Look! what an eminent work of mercy! a large sum of money given as dower to a poor girl! Look! what a meritorious fast! three days' abstinence on bread and water! *Look not on his countenance.* To the eye these seem to be great works, and yet they are accounted as nothing by God, because they were not wrought with a right intent: whereas the crust of stale bread given in the name of a disciple, and out of love to God, is rewarded with a crown of eternal glory. I am reminded, says the preacher, of a story told by John Geminiano, which is to the point.

Two women came before a judge, contending about the ownership to a clew of wool, which each claimed to be her own.

The judge inquired as to the shred upon which the wool had been wound. One woman declared she had wound it upon a bit of black rag, another affirmed that the piece was white. Then the judge ordered the wool to be unwound, and delivered it over to the woman who had asserted that she had used a black rag; for the end of the thread was found twined round a black centre.

Oh! how carefully will all excuses, all outward appearances, be wound off at the last, and the true intent within be revealed! Now every act is like a clew, and who can tell what lies at its core, and what its origin?—all that is hidden. Now self-love persuades man that his show of virtue is wound about the best intention, as a white bobbin, but too often has it been coiled about the black one of vanity or self-will.

"Let each man fear," says St. Bernard, "lest, in that searching examination, his righteousness prove to be sin." The Amalekite soldier, who dealt King Saul his death-blow, came exultingly to David expecting great reward, and lo! he received the punishment of death; in like manner will many a man at the last perish eternally who has expected to triumph. . . .

When thou appearest before God the righteous Judge, say, whose will be the works thou hast wrought? Thy studies, thy labours, thy vigils, thy cares, thy traffic, thy contracts, thy business of life, whose will they be? Works of salvation to thee, or works of avarice? All the many Sacrifices of the altar at which thou hast assisted! All the pious sermons thou hast listened to, all the alms thou hast distributed, all the penances thou hast undergone, all the Communions thou hast received, all the fasts and mortifications thou hast undertaken, all the works of mercy thou hast performed! Tell me, are they to be referred to nature or to grace, to reason or to concupiscence, to self-love or to the love of God? Tell me, are they works meriting eternal salvation, or deserving condemnation? *Whose shall those things be which thou hast provided?*

Christian soul, all this is now veiled in mystery inscrutable, but this will be made manifest before the sun, when the Judge shall call up for examination all thy works, and pronounce upon them, one after another, according to the end, according to the method, according to the intent, according to the circumstances wherewith they have been wrought.

This admirable lesson is taken from the first sermon for the Sixth Sunday after Pentecost. I will now give a sketch of one of De Barzia's complete sermons; and I shall select for the purpose one on the subject of the solemn account those will have to give who hinder others in their spiritual progress.

There are other sermons by the preacher on the same subject, but this is the best among discourses which are all very good. To my taste this sermon is superior to any by Paolo Segneri.

The text is from the Gospel for the day—with us, the Gospel for the Purification.

## The Sunday after Christmas Day.
### Sermon II.

Luke ii. 40. *And the child grew, and waxed strong in spirit, filled with wisdom; and the grace of God was upon Him.*

*Exordium.* Among other iniquities which Absalom committed in his rebellion, perhaps the chief was that he, by flatteries and fair promises, stole away the hearts of the men of Israel from their allegiance to David.

Foolish youth! exclaims the preacher; see the veterans of the king drawn up before thee in battle array! See the army of mighty warriors assembled to overthrow thee! Thy destruction impends; it is but a matter of a few hours more or less. Yet, lo! on the contrary, I see David fleeing; David, the mighty man of war; David, who shrank not before Goliath; David, who quailed not before Saul; he, even he, without striking a blow, turns his back to flee before an undisciplined rabble! How can we account for this? Chrysostom replies, "David fled, not because he feared, but because he did not choose to see his son slain before his eyes." It was love, not fear, which put him to flight. So great was the guilt of Absalom in weaning the children of Israel from their duty, that it could only be washed out in the blood of the offender. And all those who by enticing words, or by evil example, allure others from their duty to God, their true King, act as did Absalom, and like Absalom will be slain, *all the sort of them.*

*Propositio.* The subject of this sermon is the severe judgment which will fall on all those who put stumbling-blocks in the way of their brethren, or who, in any way, impede their spiritual progress.

*Confirmatio.* We do not hear of God's wrath being kindled against any nation so fiercely as against Amalek. *I will blot out the remembrance of Amalek from under Heaven,* He swore, and He bade Saul again and again, *Go and smite Amalek.* What was the sin of this people, that Divine fury should thus be roused against it? The answer is threefold.

First, the children of Amalek opposed the progress of the Israelites to the Promised Land; and Moses reminded the people that this sin was not to go unpunished: *Remember what Amalek did unto thee by the way, when ye were come forth out of Egypt; how he met thee by the way, and smote the hindermost of thee, even all that were feeble behind thee, when thou wast faint and weary; therefore it shall be, when the Lord thy God giveth thee rest from all thine enemies round about, in the land which the Lord thy God giveth thee for an inheritance to possess it, that thou shalt blot out the remembrance of Amalek from under Heaven; thou shalt not forget it.* (Deut. xxv. 17—19.)

But this is not a sufficient answer. Did not other nations rise up against Israel to withstand them in their advance? The Midianites fought against them; the Amorites blocked their way; Og, King of Basan, fell upon them; and yet against these no such fearful denunciations of wrath were launched. *The Lord hath sworn, that the Lord will have war with Amalek from generation to generation.* And four hundred years after: *Thus saith the Lord of Hosts, I remember that which Amalek did to Israel, how he laid wait for him in the way, when he came up from Egypt. Now go and smite Amalek, and utterly destroy all that they have, and spare them not; but slay both man and woman, infant and suckling, ox and sheep, camel and ass.* (1 Sam. xv. 3.) For the second reason turn to the thirty-sixth chapter of Genesis.

*Timna was concubine to Eliphaz, Esau's son; and she bare to Eliphaz Amalek.* Consequently the Israelites and the Amalekites were near of kin; they were sprung from the loins of one father, Isaac. This nation, consequently, which was bound by kindred to assist the Israelites, forgot its ties of blood, and fell upon them.

There is also a third reason for the annihilation of Amalek. It was the FIRST of all the nations to assault the chosen people, the first to fall upon them with the sword, the first to stop the way to the Promised Land. This was the final reason why Amalek was singled out for such overwhelming destruction that Balaam in prophecy could exclaim: *Amalek was the first of the nations that warred against Israel* (marg.), *but his latter end shall be that he perish for ever.* The children of Israel were in a critical position when encamped at Rephidim: they had just escaped from Egypt, and in a few days they might return thither if their hearts failed at the prospect of war. They had begun to sigh for the leeks, and the onions, and the flesh-pots of Egypt, and but little more was wanting to bring their discontent to a climax, and to send them back to their captivity. Amalek, being the first to attack them, set an example to other nations of the land, provoking Midianite, Moabite, and Amorite to regard the chosen people of God as enemies instead of treating them as wayfarers, to impede their progress instead of opening to them a passage.

*Applicatio.* From this learn, Christian soul, that if God chose to annihilate this people because it hindered the chosen race in its progress to the Land of Promise, because it opposed this people which it was bound by relationship to assist, because it was the first to do so, thereby encouraging others to stand against it—then great indeed will be God's wrath with you, if you prevent others from reaching the Heavenly Canaan, they being members of the same spiritual family, and you being the one to encourage others to destroy the souls for which Christ died.

Let infidel, heathen, and heretic persecute, their guilt is tolerable compared to yours; if you lead from the paths of righteousness, and you be the first so to lead astray, one who is of the same household of Faith, a brother, a relation, one redeemed by Christ's blood, a member of the same mystical body, of the same Church—think what you are thereby doing! Christ, the true Moses, is leading His people from the Egypt of sin, through the wilderness of this world, into the country of everlasting felicity. And what are you doing? Barring the passage to God's people, undoing the work of Christ, setting at nought the blood of the covenant. Terrible will be the condemnation of those who act thus!

De Barzia, after having appealed earnestly to the consciences of his hearers, and urged them to examine themselves whether they have ever put an occasion of falling in their brother's way, bursts into a magnificent piece of irony. He says that he hears the excuse made,—"Come, now! persecution is a strong term, unjustifiably strong; I never persecuted any one for leading a holy life: I may have teased So-and-so, but that is all; just teased him in joke, you understand." In joke! a joke more ruinous than the worst cruelty of a persecutor. A joke! Ah, ha! a right merry joke, a capital joke, indeed! Go, cut the pipes which bring water into this city—only in joke, of course—cut the pipes, then, and watch the result. Such a joke! the fountains fail, the mills cease working, the gardens are parched up, men and beasts perish through thirst. Oh, magnificent joke!

This the Bishop applies with all his vehemence and fire. He then continues by reference to the old law: *Life for life, eye for eye, tooth for tooth, hand for hand, foot for foot, burning for burning, wound for wound, stripe for stripe.* If a man smote another with a stone and injured him, by the law of Moses he was bound to pay for the cure of the injured man, and also for the loss of time. By which is signified, that if any one by evil example, or bad advice, cause spiritual sickness in another, he must atone for that, suffering for the sins which he has led his brother to commit.

*Epilogus.* Woe to such an one on the last great day, when the Judge says, "See, impious man, this child was waxing strong *in spirit, filled with wisdom, and the grace of God was upon him,* but you by your sneers and ridicule, by your jests and scoffs, turned him aside from the path of My commandments into the way of death. You have made My labours for that poor soul in vain; come now, make recompense for all that you have done," and He shall deliver him to the tormentors till he have paid the debt.

At the risk of wearying the reader, I shall give in outline a specimen of one of De Barzia's Saints'-day sermons, and I select the third for the festival of St. John the Divine.

*Text, John xxi.—What is that to thee?*

*Introduction.* Although our Lord promised to His disciples that they should have whatsoever they asked, yet He made the condition—*If ye abide in Me.* Wherefore? Judas had at this time gone out, so that those to whom the promise was made were certain to abide in Christ; and He in His foreknowledge knew that of the eleven all would remain constant till death. But Jesus spake not out of His omniscience as God, but out of care for the eleven, lest they should be elated and puffed up with spiritual pride, knowing that they were ordained to eternal life. Christ spoke conditionally, so as to teach them fear and anxiety for themselves, and in order to keep them humble.

*Subject.* The uncertainty in which we are as to our future condition is salutary; for it keeps us on the watch, it makes us cautious and anxious about our salvation.

*Confirmation.* When Jacob fled from Laban, he was pursued by his father-in-law, who had lost his household gods which Rebecca had stolen. Laban charged Jacob with the theft, and Jacob bore the charge with patience, and without resentment. But after that Laban had searched through the goods of his son-in-law, *but found them not. And then*, but not till then, *Jacob was wroth and chode with Laban.* (Gen. xxxi. 36.) How was this? At first Jacob was full of meekness, but now he is wroth. Oleaster gives the reason, he says: "At first Jacob knew not whether the idols were amongst his stuff or not, but now, the moment that he feels himself secure, his anger breaks forth against Laban for having accused him of the theft. As long as he was afraid lest the idols should be found, he was silent; but when they were not found, then he became bold." And which of you, Christian souls, knows whether some idols may not be secreted in the dark corners of your hearts, some secret sins buried deep in your bosoms? No man knoweth. Wonderful is the providence of God which leaves us ignorant as to our final condition, so as to keep us humble. But suppose now, O man! that you were assured of your final acceptance, satisfied that there was no idol hidden in the depths of your heart, would you not be filled with pride as was Jacob, would you not break forth into words of contempt for those who are not so sure?

*Epilogue.* Thanks be to Thee, O infinite God, for Thy great mercy in having veiled Thy final judgment from our eyes, so that every one is rendered fearful lest he should miss the prize of his high calling, and fail to reach the crown for which he is now striving. For Thou hast concealed it solely for our good: yet is our future state foreknown to Thee; and Thou wouldst have us serve Thee not for the hope of reward, or for the fear of torment, but from love: and Thou art worthy to be loved and served though there were no future glory, no future hell.

# JACQUES MARCHANT.

ALTHOUGH the subject of this notice was well known in his own day as an eloquent preacher, his sermons, with few exceptions, have not come to us in their original condition, and Marchant is known now chiefly as a dogmatic and moral theologian. His great work, the Hortus Pastorum, contains the notes of his sermons and catechetical instructions, as we know from his own account; and he published them in a compendious form, that they might serve the like purpose to other preachers. The Hortus Pastorum differs widely from the Dictionaries and Libraries of Predication, which issued from the press at the close of the Middle Ages; for they contained crude extracts from the Fathers and from Mediæval expositors of Holy Scripture, without any attempt being made at digesting them into a form ready for delivery, whereas each proposition of Marchant might be pronounced from the pulpit verbatim, and indeed possesses all the ring of a popular sermon.

Jacques Marchant flourished in the Low Countries at the beginning of the seventeenth century. He had the good fortune to sit at the feet of Cornelius à Lapide, when that great man taught at Louvain, a circumstance fully appreciated by Marchant, and referred to by him with thankfulness in his preface.

He was appointed Professor of Theology in the Benedictine monastery of Floreffe, which had been founded in 1121 by Godfrey Count of Namur, and he seems to have looked back in his later life with firm attachment to his cloister life in that picturesque and venerable abbey above the gliding Sambre. He was afterwards removed to the more famous monastery of Lobes, which had sent forth so many great men in the Middle Ages, and there he contracted a lasting intimacy with Raphael Baccart, afterwards its abbot.

Marchant was next transferred to the town of Couvin, to the church of which he became pastor and dean.

Jacques Marchant wrote his work, "The Garden of Pastors," at the instigation of his brother Peter, a Franciscan, at one time Commissary and Visitor-General of the Province of Britain, and afterwards Provincial of that of Flanders.

The Dean of Couvin was a man of very remarkable refinement of taste. His mind was eminently poetic, and there is not a subject which he touched, over which he has not cast a gleam of beauty. He handles his matter with the utmost tenderness, yet he holds it with the firm grasp of a theologian.

The glow of his fervent piety irradiates every page of his writings, and invests them with that peculiar charm which attaches to the works of the great mystic and spiritual writers of an earlier age. He is full of holy reverence and godly fear: with him there is none of that offensive trifling with sacred matters, none of that profane prying into solemn mysteries, which disgraced certain of the earlier preachers, who were only eager to exhibit themselves as well versed in the subtleties of the schools.

Marchant never approaches a sacred subject but with veiled face and the bow of reverence; never does he degenerate into buffoonery; "The wise man doth scarcely smile a little,"—and the smile of our author is inexpressibly sweet.

If St. Thomas Aquinas is to theology what Michael Angelo was to art, then Jacques Marchant may take his place beside Angelico of Fiesole.

And perhaps the reason of this spirituality is, that the Dean drew from the purest wells of living water, instead of letting down his pitcher in the polluted cisterns of a pagan antiquity. Profoundly learned he was not; his knowledge of the classics was but limited; —but he was well versed in the writings of the great Christian Fathers, and well trained in the science of the Saints.

His pure and loving spirit seems to have panted, like the hart, for the water-brooks of Divine wisdom, and to have turned instinctively from the dry and sterile land whither the men of his day were bending their steps. Yes; he left the satyr to dance in the desolate ruins of the olden world, that he might lie down in the green pastures of the Christian faith.

It is certainly remarkable that, whereas in his day

men affected to quote the classic writers of Rome and Greece, and the study of these authors was reviving, Marchant passes them almost completely over [1]. The catalogue of his library I give, as it would be hard to find one more judiciously selected.

His commentators on Holy Scripture, in addition to the Fathers, are Jansenius, Titelmann, Jansonius Baradius, Viegas, Salasas, Ribera, and Cornelius à Lapide. His theological writers, after the great Thomas and Cajetan, are Bellarmin, Suarez, Clarius, Torres, and Malderus. The preachers whom he consults are Pepin, Louis of Granada, Diez, Stella, Vega, Iachinus, Stapleton, Osorius, Valderama [2], Coster, Labata, and Carthagena.

His spiritual authors are Thomas à Kempis, Blosius, Harphius, Platus, Aponte, Sales, Salo, Solutivo, Roderiguez, Bruno, and Baldesanus.

His catechetical writers are Canisius, Somnius, Fœlisius, Nider, Bayus, and Claude Thuet.

"And although," says Marchant, "I may have amassed stones, wood, and mortar from other sources than my own field or quarry, in order that I might erect this edifice, yet do not deny it to be mine, for it is according to my own scheme; mine is the labour, mine the skill, mine the hand which erected, disposed, and consummated it. No one surely will deny that the garden is his who possesses, digs, cultivates, arranges, and adorns it, though he may have brought from else-

---

[1] I believe he quotes Juvenal twice, Ovid once, and the Æneid twice.

[2] Valderama, however, is not to be commended; he is vulgar, pompous, and irreverent.

where some seeds, herbs, fruit-trees, and flowers, which by pruning, lopping, and transplanting, he may have sown or planted there. However, it is little to have sown, planted, watered, and cultivated, unless there be increase and fruit produced, all which comes, not of human skill, but of God alone.

"I say, then, that the garden is not mine, but His who worketh all in all, to whom I commend and reconsecrate it with my whole heart, that He may give it increase. And do thou use it happily, and pray for me. Farewell."

The Hortus Pastorum consists of four books; the first treats of Faith, the second of Hope, the third of Charity, the fourth of Justice—the four great streams springing from one source which water the Eden of the Church.

Under the head of Faith, Marchant expounds the Apostles' Creed in seventeen tracts, each containing several propositions and lections.

Under the head of Hope, he discusses prayer, and especially the Lord's Prayer and the Angelic Salutation. In this book are five tracts.

Under the head of Charity, Marchant treats of the Commandments, in four tracts.

The fourth book of the Hortus Pastorum has a separate title, the Tuba Sacerdotalis, or the sevenfold blast of the priestly trumpet laying low the walls of Jericho.

These walls of the city of palms are, according to Marchant, the seven deadly sins, which he accordingly treats of in seven tracts, each containing from nine to ten lections.

In addition to the Hortus Pastorum and the Tuba

Sacerdotalis, Marchant is the author of other works, a list of which follows, together with the list of the different editions of the Hortus.

Hortus Pastorum; Parisiis, Soly. fol., 1638.
 Do.   do.   1651.
 Do.   do. Josse, fol., 1661.
 Do.   Coloniæ, 4to., 1643.
 Do.   nova editio curante M. Alix; Lugduni, fol., 1742.

Candelabrum Mysticum; Montibus, 4to., 1630.
 Do. cum Horto; Parisiis, fol., 1638.
 Do. do.  do.  1651.
 Do. do.  do.  4to., 1696.

Vitis florigera de palmitibus, etc.; Parisiis, fol., 1646.
Triomphe de St. Jean Baptiste; Mons, 12mo., 1645.
Opuscula pastoralia; Parisiis, 4to., 1643.
Resolutiones pastorales; Coloniæ, 18mo., 1655.
 Do.   cum Horto, q. v.

Quadriga Mariæ Augustæ; Montibus, 8vo., 1648.
Conciones funebres; Coloniæ, 2 vols. 4to., 1642.
 Do.   do.   1652.

Rationale Evangelizantium, in quo doctrina et veritas evangelica sacerdotibus ad pectus appendenda. Acc. Vitis florigera. Ed. quinta opusculis part. &c. Coloniæ, 3 vol. in uno, 4to., 1682.

The funeral orations are hardly likely to be much read now, but the sermons on the Saints, published under the title of Vitis florigera, are of value; they give an outline of the life of each Saint, and a moral application of the lesson inculcated by the Church in the appointment of the festival. The Resolutiones pastorales will be found exceedingly useful, as it contains solutions of many difficulties which are likely to beset a parish priest. The Candelabrum Mysticum is a very important and useful practical exposition of the Sacraments, and the Virga Aaronis florens, which is generally bound up with the Hortus, is an admirable directory of priestly life, containing godly admonitions and advice, under five heads and thirteen lections, each lection representing a blossom on Aaron's rod, or a perfection in the sacerdotal life to which every priest should labour to attain. At the end of this work there is an interesting account of the introduction and founding of a congregation of St. Charles Boromeo (oblates), in the diocese of Leyden, by the joint efforts of Marchant and his friends Stephen Strecheus, Suffragan of Leyden, and John à Chokier, Vicar-General. This congregation is a society of secular Clergy constituted on much the same principles as the Societies of the Oratorians and St. Philip Neri. At this time, when associations for the advancement of spiritual life are being formed in our own branch of the Church, it would be well to consider whether the rules of St. Charles might not be taken and adapted to our modern exigencies, and so the congregation of oblates be revived amongst ourselves.

But to return to the Shepherd's Garden.

As a specimen of the manner in which Jacques Marchant expounds a doctrine, I will give in outline his exposition of the eleventh Article of the Creed— "The Resurrection of the Body."

Lection I. On the resurrection of the dead.

Proposition 1. Universal resurrection was announced in the Old and New Testaments; Christ proves this from the words, *The God of Abraham, Isaac, and Jacob,* saying, *He is not the God of the dead, but of the living.*

For the Sadducees denied the existence of angel or spirit, and a state of life after death.

If God is God of Abraham, Isaac, and Jacob, and He is God of the living, then these patriarchs are in a state of existence after death.

Christ quoted from Moses, and not from passages in the prophets, because the Sadducees accepted the Pentateuch only.

Christ raised some from the dead as an earnest of what He would do hereafter, as for instance, Lazarus, the widow's son, and the daughter of Jairus.

Proposition 2. The resurrection of the body, though naturally hard to be understood, is most easy to be performed by God.

The doctrine of the resurrection was unknown to the philosophers.

There are natural difficulties in the way, yet it is possible with God, as illustrated by the vision of Ezekiel (xvii.).

Daniel also was promised the resurrection (xii. 2).

Marchant relates the story of the seven sleepers as an illustration of the manner in which those sleeping in their graves may awake in the flesh and in the likeness of their former selves.

Nature gives us figures and types of resurrection: the seeds decaying and springing up again; the trees shedding their leaves to burst again into leaf, and flower, and fruit; the waning of the year to break again into spring.

If there is a difficulty in our conceiving how a body scattered to the winds may be restored, take a globule of quicksilver, shiver it into countless minute particles, gather them again into your palm, and lo! the globule is identical with that which was before.

Proposition 3. This doctrine of a resurrection has been the source of joy and consolation to saints and martyrs in their afflictions.

Example of Job. *I know that my Redeemer liveth, and that He shall stand at the latter day upon the earth: and though after my skin worms destroy this body, yet in my flesh shall I see God.* (Job xix. 25, 26.)

Example of the seven brethren (2 Macc. vii.).
Examples of St. James and St. Nicasius.

The Apostle asserts that if we had no such hope *we should be of all men most miserable*, but we have a hope of resurrection (Phil. iii. 20, 21).

In like manner then as the husbandman (James v.) waits unconcernedly for the time when his seed sown in corruption shall spring up, so must we not be saddened if these our corruptible bodies waste and decay, but must commit them unto the faithful Creator, remembering the words of Habakkuk, *Rottenness entered into my bones, and*

*I trembled in myself, that I might rest in the day of trouble. . . . Yet I will rejoice in the Lord, I will joy in the God of my salvation. The Lord God is my strength, and He will make my feet like hinds' feet, and He will make me to walk upon mine high places.*

Lection II. Of the identity of the risen with the present body.

Proposition 1. The two bodies are essentially *one.* The resurrection is one of the flesh, not of the soul only.

It is a resurrection of substantial flesh, not of an aerial phantom.

Job distinctly says, *In my flesh shall I see God, whom I shall see for myself and not another;* in the same skin and flesh, not in other skin and flesh; with the same eyes.

Example of Eutychius of Constantinople confessing this truth when dying.

Corollary. From this we see what dignity belongs to the human body, with what reverence man should treat it, and how it is worthy to be guarded carefully by angels (Jude 9).

Proposition 2. Although the risen body is identical with the natural body in substance, yet it differs from it in accidents. For the risen body has four dowers —

    1. Impassibility, or incapacity for suffering pain, disease, or corruption.

    2. Glory, being made resplendent as the sun, after the fashion of Christ's transfiguration

3. Agility, or capacity for following every impulse of the will.

4. Subtlety, or capacity for penetrating every where.

Of these four conditions of the body the Apostle speaks (1 Cor. xv. 42—44), *It is sown in corruption, it is raised in incorruption* (impassible) ; *it is sown in dishonour, it is raised in glory ; it is sown in weakness, it is raised in power* (agile ) ; *it is sown a natural body, it is raised a spiritual* (subtle) *body.*

St. Paul takes the figure of a grain of corn, which is sown in corruption, decaying in the earth, but rises in incorruption ; and shows that in like manner will the body rise free from corruption.

The body is sown in dishonour ; however noble and illustrious it may have been in life, it becomes an object of loathing in the tomb; but it will be raised glorious, radiating light.

The body sown in weakness, unable to resist the attack of decay and the worm, will be vigorous and free on the Resurrection morn, capable of performing any act which the mind can devise.

The body sown an animal or natural body, subject to vegetative processes, and other conditions of nature, at the Resurrection will be free from all these conditions.

Proposition 3. Bodies here deformed, will hereafter be perfected.

Marchant reasons that, in a state of perfection, all imperfection, and therefore all deformity, will be done away.

He discusses the question of the age to which all bodies will seem to have attained at the Resurrection; the received doctrine being that *we* shall *all come . . . unto a perfect man, unto the measure of the stature* (marg. *age*) *of the fulness of Christ.* (Eph. iv. 13.)

Lection III. The circumstances of the resurrection.

Proposition 1. The trumpet call precedes it.

For it takes place *in a moment, in the twinkling of an eye, at the last trump*—that trump being the voice of the archangel. (1 Thess. iv. 16. Matt. xxiv. 31.)

The trumpet of old called to a solemn assembly; it was a sign of advance, it was a signal of battle. So will the last trump *call the Heaven from above and the earth, that* God *may judge His people;* it will be the sign of advance to the elect into their kingdom, it will be the signal for all creation to arm itself to fight against the ungodly.

Do you ask what is the object of the trumpet blast?

   1st. It is to call the angels together, to prepare for the severance of good and bad.

   2nd. It is to wake the dead.

   3rd. It is to summon the elect to the feast of good things in Heaven.

   4th. It is to terrify the wicked and announce to them their doom.

Proposition 2. The locality of the resurrection is uncertain.

It is supposed by many that it will take place in the Valley of Jehoshaphat, where good and bad will be gathered together. Others suppose that the good and bad will be gathered in separate spots. Others again suppose that each individual will remain by the grave whence he has arisen.

Proposition 3. The time when the resurrection will take place is also uncertain.

Some think it will take place early on Easter Day, *at the rising of the sun*, that our resurrection may be made in all points like that of our great Head. Others think that it will take place suddenly at night: *At midnight there was a voice heard, Behold, the Bridegroom cometh; go ye out to meet Him.* The type of Israel coming out of Egypt points also to midnight.

But the place and the time knoweth no man, they depend on the Providence of God.

I confess to feeling quite at a loss what to select as a specimen of Marchant's refined and beautiful writing. Every page contains beauties, and it is hard to choose among them.

The following is very tender. After quoting the text, *My beloved is white and ruddy, the chiefest among ten thousand* (Cant. v. 10), he breaks forth into the following passage: "White is my Beloved in His purity and His innocence, but ruddy in His burning charity, through which He shed His blood. White is He in His nativity, girded about with virgin flesh, but ruddy in His circumcision, sprinkled with His gore. White at the transfiguration, in His glistering raiment, ruddy on the Mount of Olives, bleeding in His sweat. White is He in the palace of Herod, dressed in the white robe, ruddy in that of Pilate in the purple garment. White upon the Cross, in the water which flowed from His side, but ruddy, bathed wholly in His Blood. White is He in the Sacrament, under the species of bread, ruddy under the veil of wine. White in His mercy, ruddy in His justice; white in His Body mystical, in the virgins, but ruddy in the purpled martyrs." (114.)

"*He is the chiefest among ten thousand*, through His passion exalted above all creatures and above all glory of the elect.

"The chiefest among ten thousand, as leader of His people Israel to the Promised Land, by the pillar, the rod, and the Red Sea; the pillar, forsooth, at which He was scourged, the rod of His Cross, and the Red Sea of His Blood.

"The chiefest among ten thousand, as the great High Priest entering into the holiest of all with His own blood.

"The chiefest among ten thousand, as the Mediator between God and man, ever presenting before the Father those wounds by which He was constituted Mediator.

"The chiefest among ten thousand, as the Shepherd of either fold, that of Jew and that of Gentile; by the pastoral staff of His Cross reducing them into one fold under one Shepherd.

"The chiefest among ten thousand, as Head of the militant and triumphant Church.

"The chiefest among ten thousand, as Head and King of angels and men, of both making one society, one kingdom.

"The chiefest among ten thousand, as the Judge of living and dead." (110.)

I make no apology for translating, almost entire, the following exquisite passage on the wound in our Lord's side, so redolent with spiritual fragrance, so rapturous in heavenly ardour:—

"Not only ought the dove to dwell in the clefts of the rock, but she should also flee to the *cavernam maceriæ* (English vers., 'secret places of the stairs'): that is, the wound in the side. . . . There make thy nest, and enter, O dove! therein lurk many mysteries: for why was that side opened?

"First, that thou mightest enter the ark with the olive-bough, the symbol of peace. Lo! Christ is the ark, and the wound in His side is the window of the ark through which thou mayest enter; for as the dove found not rest for the sole of her foot, so dost thou wander in vain with the raven, and wheel around the corpses of this world; thou canst not find thy rest, save in the heart of thy Saviour. There has He chosen to build thee a home; there, in that heart burning with love, to plant thee a flowery Paradise, in which thou mayest delight, and exclaim, *It is good for us to be here.* 'How good!' says Bernard, 'how good to dwell in that heart, in that dug field!' O Lord, Thy heart is a good treasure, for which I will surrender all my fancies, all the desires of my mind. I will acquire it for myself, casting all my thoughts into Thy heart; and I will worship toward this ark of the covenant, and praise the name of the Lord. . . . .

"If then at any time thou feelest want and lukewarmness, or dryness, then turn thy heart to the Lord, turn to the heart of thy Lord; seek it on the cross, His couch of love. There wilt thou find the way to His very heart open; by that broad gate of His side, by that door of piety, thou mayest enter. There join heart to heart, that thou mayest become partaker of light, of life, of flame, and of that peace which *He shall speak unto His people, and to His saints, that they turn not again.*

"Secondly, He chose that His side should be opened, because to the Redeemer it was not enough that His whole body was bloody with the rods, that His hands and feet were purpled by the nails, but He desired to shed forth, by the spear, as token of His unbounded love, that blood which still lingered about the heart, and which neither thorns nor scourge had extracted. Wherefore He was wounded, not so much by the spear, as by love, or if you prefer it, by both the lance and love. Whence it is said twice, *Thou hast wounded My heart, My sister, My spouse; thou hast wounded My heart!* And do thou reply, 'Wound Thou my heart, my Bridegroom; wound Thou my heart! wound it with compassion, wound it with love; with these twin arrows from Thy bow pierce through my heart. Twice did Moses smite the rock, twice do Thou smite this stony heart, that from it may stream, if not blood, yet bitter tears.'

"Thirdly, He chose to show us the place of our regeneration. Hence there flowed forth both water and blood, signs of Baptism and the Eucharist, which regenerate us to God. And thus is it said, *Thy daughters shall be nursed at Thy side* (Isa. lx. 4), O Christ! for Thou regeneratest us by the blood and water streaming from Thy side.

"Fourthly, consider that, although the lance gave no pain to the Saviour, yet was it keen, for it wounded with cruel pang the heart of the Mother. For her heart was bound up with the heart of her Son; and to this the prophet seems to refer when he says, *Supra dolorem vulnerum meorum addiderunt.* (Ps. lxix. 27.) But in conclusion, I repeat—Arise, O dove! enter in, O love! for here is the door by which thou shalt pass to the marriage-feast of thy Bridegroom; for here is the window of love which desires to enkindle thee also; for here is the furnace streaming forth with mercy. Gathering together all thy evil affections, thy sins, thy negligences, cast them into that furnace of love, that there they may be consumed. There exclaim with Thomas, *My Lord, and my God!* and with the Psalmist, *This shall be my rest for ever; here will I dwell, for I have a delight therein.* For there is the place to live, there is the place to die."

In like manner does Marchant exclaim: "Spare, O cruel nails, O spare those sacred feet, which have never walked in the way of sinners. Come rather and pierce my heart; pierce my hard heart with the piercing of penitence, that ye may draw from it the salty tears of contrition; for, from the time when ye were sprinkled with the Saviour's blood, ye have had power to heal the wounds of the mind.

"Yet would not the Saviour spare Himself these nails, that He might make satisfaction for all offences committed by our feet walking in the way of sinners, when we went astray like the lost sheep; and that He might merit by this price and these pangs to guide our feet into the way of peace.

"It was not sufficient for Him to have endured so much labour, sweat, and weariness, whilst seeking His wandering sheep; but He desired also that His feet should at length be pierced, not with the thorns only, but also with the nails."

On the words, *He stood in the midst of them*, he remarks: "There then were the disciples gathered in terror, in error, all had lost their faith, all wavered, doubting of the resurrection. All, the Virgin excepted, had lost the light of faith, as is represented by the Church in her Office for Holy Week (i. e. Tenebræ), when fifteen candles are extinguished, one alone being excepted and allowed to remain alight. This indicates the eleven Apostles with the three women losing the light of faith, which remained in the Virgin alone, of whom it might truly be said, *Her candle goeth not out by night.* These, then, being gathered together, Christ was present in the midst, though the doors were shut; for just as He issued from the Virgin's womb leaving her still virgin, as He passed through the unmoved stone of the sepulchre, so now did He enter to His disciples without impediment, for nothing can hinder the transit of a glorious body: *He stood in the midst of them!* Stood as a pastor in the midst of his flock, gathering them to him; as a leader in the midst of his soldiers, encouraging them; as the sun in the midst of the stars, illumining them; as the heart in the midst of the body, vivifying it; as the tree of life in the midst of Paradise amongst the elect trees; as the candlestick in the midst of the house, lighting it and dispelling its gloom; as the column in the midst of the building, sustaining it.

"And this word *stood* has its special significance, denoting the resurrection. For before the resurrection, when He bore the burden of our sins, He is described as at one time lying in the manger, at another as seated weary by the well, and then as prostrate with His face to the earth praying, upon the mountain, or as bowed down and crying to the Father in the garden, or again as stooping under the weight of the cross as He ascended Calvary, whilst on the cross itself He is spoken of as bowing His head to give up the ghost. All which attitudes of the body denote the weight of our sins with which He was burdened. But now, that burden is shaken off in His resurrection, for He has drowned it in the abyss of His blood, and so rightly is He spoken of as *standing* in the midst."

Jacques Marchant thus paraphrases the 110th Psalm: "At the ascension it was said unto Him, *Sit Thou on My right hand, until I make Thine enemies Thy footstool.* That is, Do Thou, who art exalted above all creatures, share with Me My kingdom until all Thine enemies are subjected unto Thee, till the kingdom of the predestinate is filled, and Thy victory has attained to its perfection. And here by the fulfilling of the kingdom of predestination, and the conquering of foes, and the extension of empire, this is signified, that in the consummation of the age, He will return again into the world, that the subjection of every thing to Him may be made manifest in all the world. Wherefore the Psalmist adds, *The Lord shall send the rod of Thy power out of Sion : be Thou ruler, even in the midst among Thine enemies.* That is, the sceptre of Thy royal power, the sceptre of strength, shalt Thou begin to extend and pass on from the city and mount of Sion, even unto the ends of the earth, by Thy Apostolic messengers; so that Thou mayest rule even in the midst of Thy enemies and false brethren, Jews, heathen, and heretics. In the end of the age, however, Thy kingdom will be exalted perfectly over Thine enemies, when Thou shalt send forth the sceptre of virtue, the banner of Thy cross out of the Heavenly Sion, that Thy foes may be entirely subjected beneath Thy feet. Then he adds: *In the day of Thy power shall the people offer Thee freewill offerings with an holy worship,* when the kingdom will be Thine, and Thine the only principality." The Vulgate varies so much from our English Version in this third verse, that Marchant's paraphrase cannot apply to it, and I shall therefore pass on to the fifth verse: " *The Lord upon Thy right hand shall wound even kings in the day of His wrath.* Christ our Lord sitting at Thy right hand shall break all the power of kings who have persecuted the Church. Then shall the Neroes, Maximinians, and Deciuses be thrust down into hell. *He shall judge among the heathen; He shall fill the places with the dead bodies:* He shall then exercise judgment over all nations, and, having condemned the wicked, shall perfect and consummate their last extermination. Then shall the *places* of hell be filled with impious men, and with devils thrust down thither and there enclosed; and that because *He shall smite in sunder the heads over divers countries,* breaking down the proud, and bringing them into confusion before all the world.

"And would you know why He is given such power to judge the nations and trample upon kings and haughty men? *He shall drink of the brook in the way: therefore shall He lift up His head.* Because, forsooth, in this way and mortal life, which glides by as a brook, He drank the turbid water, bearing our infirmities, by His Passion descending into the very depths of the stream; therefore, because of this so great humility, hath God highly exalted Him, making Him the Judge of all.

"If indeed in His first Advent it was cried, *Blessed is He that cometh in the name of the Lord; Hosanna in the highest!* how much more in that His second triumphal coming will it be cried by angels, by the elect, by kings, by priests, by people, by children, ay! by all creatures, *Let the Heavens rejoice, and let the earth be glad: let the sea make a noise, and all that therein is. Let the field be joyful, and all that is in it; then shall all the trees of the wood rejoice before the Lord, for He cometh, for He cometh, to judge the earth.*

"We too, considering that time of triumph, shall exclaim to our King and Saviour with glad accord, 'Reign even in the midst among Thine enemies! Reign, Thou Son of David, setting up Thy throne above all monarchs! Reign, Thou peaceful King, trampling under foot all the kingdom of Satan! Reign, Thou Son of Mary, in the midst of heretics and blasphemers! Reign, Thou Galilæan, in the midst of infidels once rebels! Reign, Thou Nazarene, in the midst of Julians and persecutors! Reign, Thou innocent Lamb, in the midst of ravening wolves! Reign, Thou Lamb which was slain, in the midst of angels and all the elect!' *I heard the voice of many angels round about the throne and the beasts and the elders, saying with a loud voice, Worthy is the Lamb that was slain to receive power, and riches, and wisdom, and strength, and honour, and glory, and blessing. And every creature which is in Heaven, and on earth, and under the earth, and such as are in the sea, and all that are in them, heard I saying, Blessing, and honour, and glory, and power, be unto Him that sitteth upon the throne, and unto the Lamb for ever and ever.*"

# JOHN OSORIUS.

John Osorius, a Spaniard of the diocese of Burgos, entered the novitiate of the Society of Jesus in 1558, at the early age of sixteen. He taught moral theology, but gave himself up more especially to preaching, his talents in that line soon manifesting themselves. He preached often before the Court, and was selected to deliver orations on various public occasions. For instance, he preached twice at the fitting out of the Armada, and again on its discomfiture. His three sermons, entitled *Cum nostri redirent ab Anglia re infecta*, will be found in the fourth volume of his collected sermons. He was select preacher on the anniversary of the death of St. Ignatius Loyola, the founder of his order, and also on the occasion of the death of the king. He died at Medina, aged fifty-two, in the year 1594.

His sermons have been published several times.

Concionum Joannes Osorii ; Antverpiæ, 1594-5, 3 vols. 8vo. Ibid., 5 vols., 1597, 8vo.

Concionum J. Osorii ; Colon. Hierat. 1600, 12mo., 5 vols. ; Lugduni, Pillehotte, 1601, 8vo. ; Venetiis, 1601, fol. ; Parisiis, M. Sonnium, 1601, 8vo., 5 vols. ;

Venetiis, 1604, 4to., 5 vols.; Monast. Westphaliæ, 1622, 8vo. 5 vols.

R. P. Osorii Concionum Epitome; Colon., 1602, 8vo., 3 vols.; De Sanctis, ibid., 1613, 8vo.

John Osorius was a preacher of a high order. He was eminently Scriptural, and thoroughly practical. He neither wasted his efforts on the discussion of profitless school questions, nor wearied his hearers by abstruse disquisitions on points of Canon law. His matter is always solid, and his method sound and clear. A man of refined taste and lively imagination, he could render his discourses attractive to both educated and uneducated. He seldom breaks into a torrent of eloquence, like De Barzia, but his style is polished and graceful. He had none of the fire of the Bishop of Cadiz, but in his heart burned the pure flame of a tempered zeal, not raging forth as a furnace, dazzling and scorching all around, but calmly glowing in unruffled peace, unnoticed perhaps in the glare of day, but steadily beaming as a guiding star to the wanderer in the night.

In one point he certainly resembles his countryman De Barzia, viz. in his accurate Biblical knowledge. But the use he made of Scripture was different to that made by the Bishop, as his audience was very different from that to which the Prelate addressed his Mission Sermons. Holy Scripture was the spiritual food of this Jesuit preacher, and his discourses prove his intimate acquaintance with every portion of God's Word. His discourses do not contain, as do so many modern sermons, crude and undigested lumps of Scripture, clumsily pieced and awkwardly inserted to distend the dull oration to its conventional limits, but the words of Inspiration float lightly and fragrantly on the stream of simple eloquence, as strands of new-mown grass and cut meadow flowers on the calm brook which softly glides past the field where the mowers mow the hay.

If De Barzia roused long-dead consciences, waking them from their sepulchres with note like a trumpet, bringing them forth bound hand and foot in the corpse-clothes of evil habits, and delivering them over to the confessors to be loosed and let go, Osorius quickened the consciences but just dead, with still small voice, taking them as it were by the hand and lifting them up with tenderness, that he might restore them to their parents—to their God, who was to them a Father, to the Church, which was to them a Mother.

But with all these rare merits, Osorius had his defects. His sermons are wanting in arrangement and in unity of design. He preached on the Gospel for the day, and aimed rather at giving a running commentary on the selected passage of Scripture, than at elaborating one text and concentrating his powers upon its application. Hence, each of his sermons, which are very long, may well be broken into six or eight short discourses with separate points, but when preached in their entirety the effect is that of a surfeit. Nothing can be better than the food he provides, but it is in too great abundance, and it is too varied; briefly, in his sermons there is what the French call an *embarras de richesses*.

There is this excuse to be made for Osorius, that he did but follow in the wake of the Patristic and Mediæval preachers, whose public orations consisted almost invariably of Scripture expositions, partaking more of the character of our modern Bible-class lectures than our set sermons; and it was only bold men like De Barzia, who set all conventionalities at defiance, that originated the class of sermon now recognized as the normal type of a pulpit discourse. Osorius, however, could divest himself of the trammels of custom when he chose, and he has left some notable specimens of sermons which have but one point and subject, in his fourth volume; and I very much question whether any more noble and more vigorous have ever been composed than those written by John Osorius, the Jesuit, on the Four Last Things, the Three Foes of Man, and the Seven Last Words.

Osorius seldom relates anecdotes, and his sermons are almost entirely free from those stories which preachers of his age delighted in introducing to illustrate their subjects; but, in their place, he brings forward similes to an extraordinary extent. His sermons are studded with them, and his similes are almost invariably graceful and neat. It may be questioned whether he does not somewhat overdo it, when one sermon contains fifteen similes. Yet these are so beautiful that we could ill spare one. Perhaps we are too critical in requiring all sermons to be cut to the same shape; perhaps the beauty of the wood hyacinth may consist in the multitude of its azure bells, and the splendour of the tulip would be lost if it grew in a bunch.

But the reader shall judge for himself. I will give him a string of similes from the Trinity sermons of Osorius.

"Aristotle says that as the sun, most visible in itself, cannot be contemplated without difficulty by our eyes, on account of their weakness; so God, of supreme entity and perfection, can hardly be grasped by us, through the imperfection of our intellect."

"*When my father and mother forsake me, the Lord taketh me up*, says the Psalmist; and Israel exclaimed, *Make us gods to go before us*. For without God we have not power to advance. What will he say to this, who enters on a state of life without God to lead him, who undertakes hard matters forgetful of God? As the ivy trails along the earth when it finds not a tree, to which it may cling and by which it may ascend, so does the soul lie prostrate till it has found God, to whom it may cling as to its beloved; and having found Him, by Him ascend, *going on from grace to grace*."

"*The Heavens declare the glory of God, and the firmament showeth His handiwork:* they all point wondrously to their Creator, showing themselves to be creatures fashioned by His hands.

"Cicero observes: If when travelling you came suddenly in a desert upon some magnificent palace, such as that of Solomon, and were to ask how it came thither, and the answer were made that a mountain had fallen, and that its ruins had shaped themselves, somehow, into this great mansion, you would laugh them to scorn who asserted this, for the house shows plainly the handiwork of an artificer—and that he was a famous artificer to boot—who thus ranged all in such perfect order, and this, you would say, was self-evident. So, too, he who considers the workmanship of this world with attention,—the garden of earth, the abyss of sea, the heavens wondrously adorned, the variety of stars, their varied and yet harmonious motions,—he will say that it is manifest that some master artificer has arranged them, and that their conjunction cannot be fortuitous."

"Look first at the beauteous image of the soul, and gather from it that it has a divine artificer. If you saw a boy holding a charming image in his hand, and you asked him, Whose is this image? who fashioned it? if he were to reply, I made it; you would at once say, That is not true, for it is a masterpiece of art. So, too, the wondrous power of our souls, and their wondrous perfection, point to a Heavenly artificer."

"Who, then, is God? He is One and Three: one in nature, one in wisdom, one in goodness; but three in Person: Three Persons but One God, one wise, one powerful, one good.

"How then three Persons and not three Gods? I and thou are two persons, but one in nature and species.

"How two persons with one nature? Because in me there is that which is not in thee, and this constitutes difference in personality.

"But thou sayest, What is there in the Father which is not in the Son?

"That thou mayest understand, take this illustration.

"I have invented a science, entirely of myself; this science I teach thee; thou and I communicate it to a third. The same science is in all three; one of us knows nothing which the other knows not; one knows as much as all the three. Yet is there this difference between us, I have the knowledge of myself, having received it of none; in thee it is derived from me; in the third it proceeds from thee and me. Now suppose that, instead of a science, this were my nature which I gave to thee, and which we two communicated to the third; then should we three be one in nature, and yet with the diversity I have specified.

"Thus, as I have said, is it with our God, in whom it is the same to be, to know, to be able, &c. This wisdom and nature is in the Father self-derived, received of none. It is in the Son also, the same, but received by intelligence from the Father. It is in the Holy Ghost, but proceeding from the Father and the Son by love: therefore the Persons are three, but there are not three Gods nor three Lords, for the nature, and the wisdom, and the power, and the goodness are one, but in three Persons; therefore there is but one God, one Lord, one Wise."

"God is the abyss of being, as signifies His name Jehovah; in Him are all perfections, of which perfections each is infinite, all are One. What then is my God? Ask every creature, and let them show you their God, and tell you what He is; not that each can declare Him perfectly, but each in part. Does it not happen to you sometimes, as you walk abroad, that you light upon a brook, and say, I will trace it to its source, and see whence this streamlet flows? Do you now act thus, and you will attain to your God. Mark what is good in the creatures you behold, in the song of birds, in the beauty of flowers, in the wealth of metals, in the sweetness of meats; these are but rills proceeding from God the abounding Fount; all these utter the things which are in God; for all creatures are but voices manifesting Him."

Yet we must not rest in them. "It has happened that painters have pictured fruit with such accuracy that birds have come out of the sky thinking them real, in order to feed upon them; but finding them to be painted, and that there is no food in them, they fly away to seek their true sustenance. The Divine painter has traced with His brush in His creatures the beauties which live in Himself, and in them they seem to live. Yet are they but figures, not verities, *for the fashion of this world passeth away*. Would you know how to act, knowing that these are but pictures and not realities? Act as the bird, which finding no food in the painting seeks its real meat elsewhere. Mark this, you will find in creation no true food, no satiety, no repose; mark this and fly away to your God, He is very good, He is true food, in Him alone is repose."

"When you hear sweet harmony, you say, I hear musicians, though you see them not; so seeing the harmony of creation, acknowledge God its source. In God are all perfections. Take the opal. Look at it fixedly from one point; it is white as snow, and you see nought save whiteness in it. Turn a little aside; it flashes out in flames as a carbuncle. Look from another point, it glows a rich crimson as the ruby; again, from another point it is all green as the emerald. Lo! you have an image of God, that most precious gem, to win which we must sell all we have. He is one, yet manifold. Moses beheld God, and He was to him like to the carbuncle, a burning fire: *The Lord thy God is a consuming fire.* That same God did David behold: *The Lord is full of compassion and mercy: long-suffering and of great goodness.* To him then was He not all white? Isaiah beheld him: *Wherefore art Thou red in Thine apparel?* and seeing Him executing vengeance, He was like to the ruby. John beheld Him, and *a rainbow round about the throne, in sight like unto an emerald.* Lo! what variety, and yet what unity!"

One of the most curious ideas of Osorius is the following. He says that as he lies in bed he hears the stroke, stroke, of his heart; and it sounds to him as though within were two wood-cutters engaged night and day in hewing down a tree. Nor am I wrong in thinking so, he continues, for Flux and Reflux are engaged every hour in laying their axes to the root of the tree of life. In another sermon he speaks of men fretting over the loss of worldly goods and neglecting their eternal inheritance as resembling the little boy who has built a mud castle, and who weeps when a passer-by overthrows it with his foot, though he cares nothing that a lawsuit is going on at the time by which a large inheritance is being wrested from him.

The following is singularly beautiful, to my mind. Osorius is speaking of the dower Christ has given to His Church. He says, that as when a traveller marries a wife in a far country he gives her a few presents, but says to her, O my beloved, when we come home to my own country, where all my wealth and property are, then you shall have ten thousand times better presents; so does Christ act with His Church. Here, in the *far country* of this earth, He gives her a few gifts and graces, but when He leads her home to His heavenly habitation, He will crown her with endless glory.

On the subject of the Ascension, he observes, very gracefully, that when a fleet is tossing on the sea, if one vessel enters the port in safety, the others pluck up courage to follow. When the soldiers see their leader mount the wall of the besieged city, they, though below, are stirred to press onward too.

And again, speaking of Christ resuming His seat in Heaven, he says that when a costly gem is given to a king, he sets it in a golden ring, which is exquisitely wrought, and which seemed a miracle of perfection before the insertion of the gem. But when the jewel is set, its glory eclipses all the graving of the ring. So was Heaven beauteous without Christ, beauteous as the setting, but now the precious gem, for whom all was made, is again in His place, and eclipses all other glories in His own effulgent beauty.

"The joy of Heaven must have been great, and the cause of the joy is manifest. Heaven has received its sun, enlightening it more than all its stars. It has gotten its precious gem adorning that ring of eternity more than its fine gold, more than all the comely forms thereon engraved. But, earth, how canst thou rejoice this day, deprived of the sun which late illumined thee? When the sun shines in this hemisphere, all things rejoice receiving light from it; but when it retires to the other hemisphere, those things which are in it begin their rejoicing, whilst those which are in ours are veiled in darkness, and droop in gloom and tears. When the ark of God was brought to Bethshemesh, that is, the house of the sun, the calves of the cows which drew it were shut up at home, and they lowed because the mothers which gave them milk were away. This day is the ark of God, which has been held captive in the house of this world, brought back into Heaven, the true house of the sun. And we, as the calves, remaining shut up in this world's tabernacle, without our nourishment from the breast and wounds of Christ, how shall we do otherwise than low and lament?"

This beautiful and quaint passage will show how Osorius finds illustration in Scripture. I translate a few more specimens of his style.

"*Behold how He loved him.* St. Thomas explains this passage admirably when he says, quoting the wise man, *Nothing doth countervail a faithful friend, and his excellency is invaluable,* for a faithful friend is worthy of love: and yet, *a faithful man who can find?* He is a faithful friend who is stable in friendship; not forgetting a first friend when a new one arrives, nor when exalted in prosperity forgetful of the friend in poverty, nor despising the friend who is cast down.

"God will be found the most faithful friend, in that He never forgets former friends for the sake of new ones; but those whom He chose before time was, these will He love in eternity, when time is no more. Neither does the addition of new friends make the former less the friends of God, but rather the more grateful is it to Him that many should love Him.

Nor is Christ like the chief butler, who, when things went well with him, forgot Joseph; but *though the Lord be high, yet hath He respect unto the lowly.* Christ, when mortal, chose men to be His friends; when made immortal, He called them His brethren. *Go to My brethren, and say unto them,* &c. (John xx. 17). Nor is the friendship of Christ capable of change through loss of the friend, as is evident from the eleventh chapter of St. John. *Now Jesus loved Martha, and her sister, and Lazarus,* when they were hale and sound. But what will He do when Lazarus is sick? *Lord, behold he whom Thou lovest is sick;* He ceases not to love because His friend is sick. Lazarus dies, the misery increases, but friendship does not decrease; for He says, *Our friend Lazarus sleepeth.* Lazarus is not called friend because that he loves, but because he is still beloved. Now Lazarus stinketh, and still Christ is his friend, for He weepeth because of him. *Behold, they say, how He loved him!* Ill, O multitude, do you speak! to Him love is present, therefore rather say, Behold how He loveth him! O most faithful Friend, Thou art He who sayest, *I have loved thee with an everlasting love!*

"Far otherwise are we toward Christ. He is in bonds, and lo! Peter swears that he knows Him not. O man! if you seek a true friend, seek first Christ, who changeth not. What think you is the friendship of the world? What the friendship of the flesh? You have three friends. You are in peril, for you are summoned before the king to be tried, and sentenced for high treason. You go to your first friend, and tell him your danger, and ask of him assistance. He replies that he will accompany you as far as the judgment hall, and leave you there. 'Do you settle your affair with the king; I can do no more for you.' Seeing that there is no help to be gotten from this friend, you turn to the second, and ask of him succour. He replies, 'When you are executed, I will wrap your body in some old and cast-off linen, for a shroud.' You go to the third, and he says, 'I will be your advocate. I will assist you, and will liberate you. I will pacify the king, and, if need be, I will die in your room.' Is not this a faithful friend? Now those who enter into compact of friendship with their flesh, which of these friends have they got? The first, which will accompany you only to the gate of death. Cherish the flesh, love it, and it will be a Delilah to you, handing you over to your enemies, leaving your soul before the Judge, without accompanying it. The world resembles the second friend, to please which you must torture yourself, but all it will give you in the end will be the shroud to enwrap your dead body. But Christ is the third friend, the faithful one, our advocate, who, to liberate us, endured death for us; He who accompanies us to the judgment, who frees us, who protects us! Let Him be our friend who truly loves us. *We love God because He first loved us.*"

I conclude with the following striking passage:—

"*Are ye able to drink of the cup that I shall drink of?* Being desirous of alluring His disciples to drink of the cup, He expounds to them its sweetness, when He says that He will drink of it first. And, in sooth, if we were faithful to God, this reason would be sufficient to make us drink it readily. But, as says the wise man, *most men will proclaim every one his own goodness: but a faithful man who can find?* There is not a son, there is not a servant, who acts as faithlessly with his father or his master as we act towards God. Would you know that of a certainty? I tell you be loth to sin, be ready to die rather than sin.

"Ah! but you say, I like to sin. I ask you, Upon what grounds do you persist in sinning? Well, you say, God is so good; He loves me, He is ready to pardon. So this is the reason why you continue in sin! And what though you know this for certain, where is your fidelity? where is your Christian honour? Does a wife act in this manner with her husband? a son with his father? a servant with his lord? I pray you bid your wife act in this manner towards you. Say to her, 'Be chaste.' She will say, 'That is no concern of mine. I know full well that you are good, that you love me, and that if I were an adulteress you would pardon me.' And if it were so, would this answer of your wife gratify you? Why! where would be the honour of a good woman? where her fidelity? Would it be deemed sufficient by you, if she were an adulteress and were reconciled to her husband? Does any minister act thus? You say to the royal minister, 'Beware lest thou plot treason against your master.' He replies, 'He is an excellent king; he loves me, he will most certainly pardon me even if I do turn traitor.' O vilest of men! O man truly without honour! where is the fidelity which you owe to your monarch?

"Vilest Christian of the household of Faith, unfaithful and destitute of honour! how continue to sin? how do you still commit adultery against God? how are you so traitorous to your King? You say: He will pardon me. Be it so. Yet where is your fidelity? where your honour? Is it sufficient to be reconciled, to be a pardoned traitor? Is it not far better to be able to say, I never was a traitor?

"Now let us turn to the subject. If we are faithful servants of God, enough for us that He has said, *The cup that I shall drink of*, to make us thirst for that cup. He drank thereof before thee; wilt thou not quaff of it out of love for Him? Is there a faithful soldier who would see his sovereign enter the battle, and fight amongst the foe, and withdraw himself, leaving his king alone, and betake himself to his sports? Hear what Uriah said, *The ark, and Israel, and Judah, abide in tents; and my lord Joab, and the servants of my lord, are encamped in the open fields; shall I then go into mine house?* How different also she who said, *My Beloved is mine, and I am His.* Bernard says, 'In no other way can man respond to his God in these same words, except by love, and by drinking of the cup.' God gives thee gifts; thou canst give Him nothing. *I will take no bullock out of thine house.* God beatifies thee; thou canst not beatify Him, except by love and suffering. God loves thee; love Him thou canst. He suffered for thee; suffer for Him thou canst. Thus mayest thou render unto Him what thou hast received of Him, and return, as it were, like for like to thy God."

# MAXIMILIAN DEZA.

MAXIMILIAN DEZA, an Italian, was born in 1610, and joined the Congregation of the Mother of God, in which he soon became famous as a preacher. He seems to have been a man of fervent piety and Apostolic zeal. He had acquired a good knowledge of the Latin classics in his early years, and this he was fond of exhibiting, with some pedantry, in his discourses. But such was the taste of the times, when classic literature and art were deluging Europe, and producing a revulsion in all the laws of taste which had regulated the mediævals. This affectation of classic learning was the bane of Deza's oratory, and it is constantly obtruding itself on the reader, in a marked and offensive manner, though nowhere perhaps so prominently as in his sermon at the marriage of the Queen of Poland with the Duke of Lorraine, in the Cathedral of Neustadt in Austria, in which sermon, for instance, he enumerates celebrated marriages, as those of Cadmus and Harmonia, Jupiter and Juno, David and Michal, Isaac and Rebecca, and that at Cana—all in one breath.

As soon as his fame was established, he was in request throughout his native land, and we find him preaching at Bonona, Turin, and Milan. In 1664 he preached before the Doge at Genoa; in 1666 he was in Malta. We have sermons of his delivered at Rome in 1672, and at Venice in 1686. There is extant a sermon by Deza on the birth of the Prince of Wales, the so-called "Pretender," son of James II., and an oration preached at Venice on the occasion of the exhibition of the Blessed Sacrament for obtaining success against the Turks, with whom the Republic was then at war. Maximilian Deza was sent for by Leopold I. to preach before him at Vienna, and there the old man died peacefully in his seventy-seventh year, A.D. 1687.

His sermons were published in Italian, "Prediche dell' Avvento del P. Massimiliano Deza, Lucchese della Congregatione della Madre di Dio," by Nicolo Pezzana, Venice, 1709.

There is also a Latin edition, translated by Cassimir Moll, a Benedictine, published by Veith, Vienna, 1726, and dedicated to John Julius de Moll, Archbishop of Salzburg.

The sermons extant form three series; the first consists of sermons from the First Sunday in Advent to the Sunday after Christmas, together with two discourses on the parable of the Prodigal Son, in all nine, forming one volume. The second contains thirty-eight sermons preached during Lent; and the third part, which is immeasurably inferior to the other two, consists of orations on divers saints, such as St. Catharine of Bologna, St. Peter of Alcantara, St. Rosa of Lima, together with sermons on state occasions.

Maximilian Deza just escaped being a really great orator, like Segneri, whom he much resembles in his vehemence, zeal, fine word-painting, and brilliant transitions. There is nothing heavy or dull about his sermons; they are calculated to rivet the attention of an audience, and they appeal earnestly to the conscience. They are not sermons to be read in measured tones from the pulpit, but to be declaimed with flashing eye, modulated voice, and vehement gesture. To modern readers Deza seems to play with an idea in a manner unsuitable to our nineteenth century ideas of pulpit proprieties; but it must be borne in mind that his discourses are long, lasting sometimes two hours, and the mind of the hearer would need rest, it would only be fatigued if kept constantly on the stretch. Viewed thus, it will be seen that Deza handles his matter with great skill; he works one point of his subject to a climax, —you hold your breath even in reading him—and then he gently drops the point, and gives time for relaxation of the attention till he deems it fit to produce another effect, just as in a drama the sensational scenes are separated from each other by the talkee-talkee scenes in the front groove. But these intermediate portions of Deza's sermons are by no means dull; they are light and pleasant trifles with which he toys, but which lead on insensibly to his point, just as the small beads of a rosary draw the fingers on to the larger ones.

Take his sermon for Ash-Wednesday as an example.

He is preaching on the words, "Remember, O man, that thou art dust, and that into dust thou shalt return," which occur in the Roman Office for the day.

He begins with the lessons drawn from the ashes sprinkled every where; and he bids his hearers look on these ashes, and remember that they shall one day be like them. He then draws with skill a picture of man's forlorn condition, with the prospect of death before him, and no possibility afforded him of escape. He laughs to scorn the thoughts of immortality connected with name and title; he tells the story of Empedocles seeking an immortal name by jumping into the crater of Ætna; and then he warns his hearers most solemnly to keep death ever before their eyes. Remember, he cries, that you have sucked in with your mother's milk the seeds of death. Remember that all beasts were created alive, but Adam was created a lifeless frame, till God breathed into his nostrils the breath of life. Remember that from the moment of birth, the moment of death began to creep nearer. Then suddenly pointing to the hour-glass he exclaims, Look ! this hour is stealing away in grains of dust, warning you to remember what you too ere long will become. And having worked this out with great solemnity, he suddenly breaks off into a description of glass and its manufacture. He says it is made of sand and ash, it is fused with heat, it is formed by the breath.

Is not that like man? he asks; man made of dust, kindled by the glow of life, vivified by the Divine breath?

Well! you will say that glass is a very brittle affair; it somewhat resembles ice, and is just as fragile; one little fall, and it is shivered into countless fragments; it is made by a puff, it is clouded by a breath, it is broken by a touch.

You consider it very fragile.—I tell you, on the authority of St. Augustine, that man is far more fragile.

Glass carefully preserved may become an heirloom, but man can never last out more than a generation.

Glass is only shattered by accident, but man is perishable by his nature.

Glass is broken by external force, but man bears about within him the seeds of dissolution.

Glass is snapped by a touch, but man untouched will crumble into his grave.

Glass once broken may be restored, not so man.

Glass though broken does not decay, but man's flesh becomes corrupt.

Having thus amused and rested his hearers, Deza begins another earnest appeal to them; he explains that the soul of man does not descend to the grave, and he solves a difficulty in the text, Genesis iii. 19, *Dust thou art, and unto dust shalt thou return.*

Having done this, it is proper that the congregation should be given a little breathing-time, and so the preacher takes the sentence, *Dust thou art,* and plays with it, by giving a description of dust agitated by the wind. Oh, into what fantastic shapes does the wind whirl the dust! how the dust-cloud runs along, rushes forward madly, stops and spins awhile, and tosses itself up, up, till it seems verily to fly; it ascends higher and higher, it is carried above the tree-tops, it will reach the clouds of Heaven. Stay!—the wind drops. Where is the dust? It falls, it obscures the landscape, it is scattered every where, it parches the tongue, it blinds the eyes, it clogs the throat; and that which just now dulled the air and obscured the sun, has returned to itself again; dust it was, and nothing more, and unto dust has it returned.

Is not this a picture of man? asks the preacher; man, poor dust carried up and hurried forward by the winds of his vain fancies? Ambition puffs him up on high, only to fling him to earth again; passion drives him forward, and then drops him a helpless atom to his native soil.

Look how high those giddy particles are flung— *Thou takest away their breath, they die, and are turned again to their dust.*

Yes, toss yourselves in pride, rush on in the storm of passion, eddy up in the struggle of life, spin in the giddiness of pleasure, penetrate every where in the eagerness of curiosity—*Thou takest away their breath, they die, and are turned again to their dust.*

Deza then examines the words of Solomon, *There is a time to be born and a time to die*, and he asks why the King did not say there is a time to live. Having answered this question to his own satisfaction, by showing that Solomon spoke of definite moments of time, but that life was not a point of time, but a fleeting succession of moments, he enters on the subject of the shortness of time, and quotes Wisdom v. 10. The life of man, says Solomon, is *as a ship that passeth over the waves of the water*, and leaves no trace—no trace but the foam-bubbles; and those foam-bubbles are like the life of man, now appearing in the wake of the vessel, and then brushed away by the next wave,—and this wave is like the life of man, sweeping on resistlessly to the rock on which it will be shivered with a roar—a roar like the life of man, loud and fierce for the moment, and then carried off on the wind—the wind like the life of man sinking into a lull and lost.

And so throughout the sermon.

I will now give an analysis of one of Maximilian Deza's most characteristic and striking discourses, with a translation of a portion of it as a specimen of his style of oratory.

The sermon I have selected is that for the First Sunday in Advent, with which the Feast of St. Andrew coincided. The lessons from each holiday are very happily blended.

Maximilian Deza takes two texts, the first from the twenty-first chapter of St. Luke, *Then shall they see the Son of Man coming in a cloud with power and great glory;* and the second from the Office for St. Andrew's Day, "Blessed Andrew prayed, saying, Hail, good Cross! may He receive me by thee, Who by thee redeemed me."

Introduction.

> On this coincidence of holidays two points of consideration are presented to us; the Cross the sign of terror and destruction to the guilty, and the Cross the sign of joy and salvation to the just.

I. The love of the Cross is the characteristic of the elect; whilst the hatred of the Cross is the sign of the reprobate.

a. The Lord knoweth those that are His— by their love of His Cross of suffering. *If any man will come after Me, let him deny himself, and take up his cross, and follow Me.*

β. But the wicked are called *the enemies of the Cross of Christ, whose end is destruction.*

The day will come, the great and terrible day of the Lord, when He will call the heavens from above, and the earth, that He may judge His people; when the Cross, the sign of the Son of Man, will appear in the clouds of Heaven.

II. Then God will judge the world with fire, and the Cross alone will be the standard by which all will be tried.

God will judge the world with fire.—How with fire? When a palace is destroyed by the flames, every thing in it is reduced to cinder; the rags of the beggar, the gorgeous robes of the prince, the statue of the king, and the image of the ape. So every man will be tried with fire, and all difference between man and man as now existing will be rendered indistinguishable. King and subject, master and slave, will stand shivering in nakedness beside each other; there is no respect of persons with God, they will be but as a heap of cinders, which are equally hideous, though some may be the ashes of costly articles, others of vile materials.

One alone distinguishing mark will be left, the love of the Cross, by which to judge them.

III. By the Cross will the saints be recognized, as in Ezekiel ix. the prophet saw in vision the destruction of the last day, when God's command was, *Slay utterly old and young, both maids, and little children, and women: but come not near any man upon whom is the mark Tau.*

This Tau, Deza observes, is the Cross, the mark on the brow by which the faithful shall be known. Tau is the last letter of the Hebrew alphabet, and it is the last sign which shall appear in Heaven. The preacher then goes through the list of those slain, old and young, maids, and little children, and women, and shows how that wisdom of grey hairs, or innocency of childhood, or purity of virgins, are of no avail to stand the fire of trial unless the Cross be the source of those graces.

The Cross is the banner of the King in His army on earth. It is the tree of life in the Paradise of His Church.

IV. The Cross, as sign of safety to some and of destruction to others, was prefigured in the Old Testament—

    *a.* By the rod of Moses, which opened the sea for the passage of the Israelites, and which brought it back again to overwhelm the Egyptians.

    β. By the ark of Noah.

    γ. By the blood-marks on the lintel and doorpost when the destroying angel passed through Egypt.

V. A contrast is drawn between St. Peter and the penitent thief. The former feared the Cross, and when our Lord spoke of His approaching crucifixion, the Apostle said, *Be it far from Thee;* and was therefore suffered to fall. But the thief who sought Christ through the Cross found acceptance.

VI. Deza shows that people may now become enemies of the Cross of Christ—

    *a.* By gluttony and drunkenness.

    β. By debauchery and frivolity.

    γ. By injustice and dishonesty.

    δ. By falsehood and calumnies.

    ε. By hypocrisy.

    He draws a very solemn and awful picture of the dawning of the great day, and the flashing of the sign of the Son of Man upon the enemies of the Cross of Christ, and then—

VII. He comments on the sentences pronounced on the good and on the bad. This is the passage I translate.

Part II.

    VIII. Maximilian Deza now shows how St. Andrew is a blessed child of the Cross. He shows how that to him the Cross was as a second mother, guiding him through life, sustaining him and embracing him in death.

IX. The love of Christ's Cross regenerates us, assures us of our sonship, and is an earnest of our inheritance.

At our birth into this world we are placed in divers positions by the will of God and by no appointment of our own. So some are born to be kings, some to be slaves, some to be philosophers, others to be fools.

But at the regeneration it will not be so. Our position then will be regulated by our own selves, for we shall be nearer to, or more remote from, Christ; be princes or subjects according to our love for the Cross of Christ during our earthly existence, according to the closeness of our walk in the bloody footprints of our Master, bearing our crosses after Him, in the season of our probation.

And in conclusion, Deza makes an eloquent and earnest appeal to his hearers to *redeem the time because the days are evil.*

The following is a translation of the seventh section of this most striking sermon, which exhibits at the same time his power and his weakness, his merits and his defects:—

"Behold!" will say the Judge, with threatening voice, to that great throng of accused; "behold! on this Cross

I poured forth all the treasures of My love—producing blood for your welfare; to you though was that most precious stream counted but as dung, squandered recklessly for some fleeting vanity. From this My Cross with last and dying voice, with tears breathing nought but piety, I called you to penitence, but as deaf adders you stopped your ears and hardened your hearts to the sweet incantations of love. On this Cross, full of sorrows and of confusion, painfully I suffered death, that I might recover eternal life for your souls; and you, meanwhile, before the countenance of God dying for you, did laugh with the scribes, mock with the Pharisees, sport with the soldiers. This My Cross was a noble pulpit from which I, the Master of humility, of patience, and of charity, taught you the love of your enemies, praying to the Father for My foes and My persecutors. But you! what did you take in, what did you learn? Answer, what? The implacable madness and rage of a Saul, the boastings of a Goliath, the impieties, and crimes, and vengeance of a Cain, a Joab, or an Absalom. And what! were your hopes too rash to calculate on finding safety in that Cross? Ah, wretched ones! Are ye not those to whom the withering roses of this world were more acceptable than My thorns? Are ye not those who sucked in the sweet poison from the cup of Babylon, but rejected the chalice of My passion? Are ye not those who, fleeing the embrace of My Cross, rushed into the arms of lust which polluted you, of the world which betrayed you, of Satan who erects his trophies upon your ruin? These, these were your lovers, these the idols of your heart, these the deities ye idolatrously worshipped—commend yourselves now to them, let them arise and help you. In Me remains no hope for you, no more bowels of mercies,—Depart from Me, ye cursed! This Cross is your condemnation; this gallows-tree is your scourge, this wood will rack and consume you more fiercely than the flames of hell. Depart from Me, ye cursed, into everlasting fire."

But oh, happy elect! to whom on the contrary the holy Cross has been the bow of peace eternal, the ladder of Heaven, the pledge of glory, the unfading palm of lasting triumph. "Come, ye blessed of My Father!" Oh, sweet words! best-loved invitation! most pleasant reception, long-looked-for glimpse of Paradise so near! "Come, ye blessed of My Father. Ye innocents by your sweat, ye penitents by your tears, ye martyrs by your blood, did water the tree of My Cross; come now, gather the fruits of safety, life, and happy immortality. Come, ye blessed of My Father. Ye who followed My blood-stained traces up the hill of Calvary, even ye shall ascend with Me to the topmost height of the heavenly Sion, where this Cross is exalted to be the trophy of your victories. Come, inherit the kingdom prepared for you from the foundation of the world. By nature were ye My subjects, but by grace My sons; and as sons of a reigning Father My kingdom shall be your patrimony, and My Cross the sceptre of a deathless realm. My charity bore it, out of love for you; your gratitude bore it, out of love for Me; now has come the season for both Me and you, that to patient love should succeed love beatifying. As long as I am God, that is, for eternity, ye shall also be happy, shall be likewise glorious, triumphant, princes of Heaven with starred diadem on your brows, and monarchs of the universe."

# FRANCIS COSTER.

THE subject of this memoir was born at Malines in the year 1531; he was one of the first to join the new Society of Jesus, and at the age of twenty-one was received into it by the illustrious founder himself.

St. Ignatius soon discovered the remarkable talents and the deep spirituality of the young man, and he stationed him at Cologne, placing him in the van of the army of the Church, and in the thick of the fight then waging between Catholics and Protestants. He was admirably adapted for his position, and fully justified the confidence placed in him by Loyola. The Lutherans and Calvinists found in him an enemy of no ordinary power, and quite invulnerable to their blows. His knowledge of Scripture was as thorough as, and was sounder than, their own. Their arguments were dissected, and the fallacies exposed, by Coster, in a manner so clear and so conclusive that he stung them to madness.

Volume after volume passed through the press from his pen, many of them composed in the vernacular, so as to be read by the vulgar. He is said to have brought back multitudes to the Church who had fallen away at the first blush of Protestantism, and to have strengthened numerous souls which wavered in doubt.

He taught astronomy and lectured on the Holy Scriptures in Cologne. He was afterwards Rector of several Colleges, thrice Provincial, and present at three General Congregations of the Order.

After a life of controversy, yet with a soul full of peace and goodwill to men, Francis Coster entered into his rest in 1619, aged eighty-eight years; of which he had spent sixty-seven in the Society of Jesus. He died at Brussels.

His works are too numerous for me to give a list of them here. A complete catalogue will be found in the *Bibliothèque des Écrivains de la Compagnée de Jésus, par Aug. et Alois Backer*, vol. i. pp. 218—224. I mention the sermons alone.

R. P. Costeri Conciones in Evangelia Dominicalia a Dom. Adventus usque ad initium Quadr.; Coloniæ, Ant. Hierat. 1608, 4to. Conciones ab initio Quadr. usque ad Domin. SS. Trinitates; ibid. id., 1608, 4to. Conciones a Domin. post Fest. SS. Trinit. usque ad Adventum; ibid. id., 1608, 4to.

R. P. Fr. Costeri Conciones in Evangelia; ibid. id., 1613, 4to.; 1626, 8vo., 3 part., 4 vol. This last the best edition.

Vyftien Catholiicke Sermoonen op t'Epistelen end Evangelien; Antwerp, 1617, fol., 4 vols.

Catholiicke Sermoonen op alle de heylichdaghen des jaers; Antwerp, 1616, fol., 2 vols.

Sermoonen op d'Epistelen van de Sendaghen,—met twee octaven; Antwerp, 1616, fol.

Francis Coster differs in style from all the other preachers whom I have quoted. He is neither eloquent nor impressive as a speaker, he is immensely long, and must have been desperately tedious in the pulpit; and yet I question whether a priest could possess a more valuable promptuarium for sermon composition or catechetical lecture than Coster's volumes. Coster is rather an expositor of Scripture than a preacher; his insight into the significance of the sacred utterances is perfectly marvellous.

Coster relates numerous stories of different merit and point. He seldom indulges in simile. He says sharp and *piquant* things in a quiet unassuming manner; and unless the reader is quite on the alert, he may miss some very happy remark couched in a few pregnant words. For instance: he says on the subject of Profession not Practice, that Christ lived thirty-three years on earth, and He did many great works; but we know of only one sermon that He preached. The arms are long, the tongue is short; the hands are free, the tongue confined behind the prison bars of the teeth; to teach us that we should work freely, but talk little. Those who profess great things and practise little what they profess are in a bad spiritual condition; the clock whose hand stands at one whilst the clapper goes twelve, is wrong in the works.

The stories Coster tells are very unequal. There is one delightful mediæval tale reproduced by him which I shall venture to relate, as it is full of beauty, and inculcates a wholesome lesson. There is a ballad in German on the subject, to be found in Pocci and Görcs' *Fest Kalender*, which has been translated into English and published in some Roman children's books.

The story was, I believe, originated by Anthony of Sienna, who relates it in his Chronicle of the Dominican Order; and it was from him that the preachers and writers of the Middle Ages drew the incident. With the reader's permission I will tell the story in my own words, instead of giving the stiff and dry record found in Coster.

There was once a good priest who served a church in Lusitania; and he had two pupils, little boys, who came to him daily to learn their letters, and to be instructed in the Latin tongue.

Now these children were wont to come early from home, and to assist at mass, before ever they ate their breakfast or said their lessons. And thus was each day sanctified to them, and each day saw them grow in grace and in favour with God and man.

These little ones were taught to serve at the Holy Sacrifice, and they performed their parts with care and reverence. They knelt and responded, they raised the priest's chasuble and kissed its hem, they rang the bell at the sanctus and the elevation; and all they did, they did right well.

And when mass was over, they extinguished the altar lights, and then taking their little loaf and can of milk, retired to a side chapel for their breakfast.

One day the elder lad said to his master—

"Good father, who is the strange child who visits us every morning when we break our fast?"

"I know not," answered the priest. And when the children asked the same question day by day, the old man wondered, and said, "Of what sort is he?"

"He is dressed in a white robe without seam, and it reacheth from his neck to his feet."

"Whence cometh he?"

"He steppeth down to us, suddenly, as it were from the altar. And we ask him to share our food with us: and that he doth right willingly every morning."

Then the priest wondered yet more, and he asked, "Are there marks by which I should know him, were I to see him?"

"Yes, father; he hath wounds in his hands and feet; and as we give him of our food, the blood flows forth and moistens the bread in his hands, till it blushes like a rose."

And when the master heard this, a great awe fell upon him, and he was silent awhile. But at last he said gravely, "Oh, my sons, know that the Holy Child Jesus hath been with you. Now when He cometh again, say to Him, 'Thou, O Lord, hast breakfasted with us full often, grant that we brothers and our dear master may sup with Thee.'"

And the children did as the priest bade them. The Child Jesus smiled sweetly, as they made the request, and replied, "Be it so; on Thursday next, the day of My ascension, ye shall sup with Me."

So when Ascension Day arrived, the little ones came very early as usual, but they brought not their loaf, nor the tin of milk. And they assisted at mass as usual; they vested the priest, they lighted the tapers, they chanted the responds, they rang the bell. But when the Pax vobiscum had been said they remained on their knees, kneeling behind the priest. And so they gently fell asleep in Christ, and they with their dear master sat down at the marriage supper of the Lamb.

This story reminds me of another, to be found in one or two mediæval sermons.

A little boy once made an agreement with an aged priest that they should say Prime together.

So, on the first morning after the arrangement, the child rose, and descended to the church, where he lighted the candles. He waited long for the priest, and pulled the bell; but the old man turned in his bed and would not rise. Then the lad looked from the window, and the land was dumb with snow. He thought, I will run forth, and sport in the snow, for the father comes not to Prime. But he resisted the temptation, and he recited the office by himself in choir.

On the second morning he descended again, and rang the bell, and lighted the tapers; but the priest came not. Then the boy thought, I will go forth and slide on the frozen pond. But he overcame the temptation, and recited the office by himself in choir.

On the third morning he turned in his bed, and thought, It is so cold, I will not rise; the father will not leave his bed, nor will I. But he resisted the temptation to lie in bed, he dressed and came down to the church, he pulled the bell, he lighted the tapers; but the priest came not, so he sang the office by himself in choir.

And this continued for six mornings; each morning

was the child tempted, each morning did he overcome the temptation. Each morning the priest lay in bed, and the little boy sang the office by himself in choir.

On the seventh morning the priest was roused by the bell, but he turned in bed and fell asleep again. Then he had a dream. He beheld in his dream the Lord Jesus standing by the treasury in Heaven; and in His hand He bare seven crowns of pure gold. "Oh, my Lord, are these for me?" exclaimed the sleeper. "Nay!" replied the Blessed One, "not for thee, but for thy little acolyte. Seven times has he been tried, and seven times has he overcome; therefore have I prepared for him seven crowns. *Blessed is the man that endureth temptation, for when he is tried he shall receive the crown of life.*"

But leaving these stories, let us turn to a sermon of Coster's, and analyze it thoroughly. It will be seen how pregnant it is with thought, how exhaustive it is as a commentary on a passage of Scripture, how suggestive it is of matter for a modern preacher.

I shall choose the sermon for the First Sunday in Lent, curtailing it in only a few points, where the conclusions drawn seem unwarranted, or where the doctrine enforced is distinctively Roman. These omissions I have made from no wish to misrepresent the preacher, but simply to reduce the bare skeleton of the sermon to moderate limits, the entire discourse filling forty-seven pages of quarto, close print, double columns, and occupying about 5000 lines. I tremble to think of the time it must have taken to deliver, if it ever were delivered.

First Sunday in Lent. Lessons from the Gospel.
Matt. iv. *And Jesus was led by the Spirit into the wilderness.*
He was *led.* Here note—
1. That God is our leader into all good works.
2. That He leads, but does not constrain.

*By the Spirit.* Here note—
1. That in our Lent fast, we should follow the Spirit's leading. Now the Spirit leads and guides—
   α. By the voice of the Church.
   β. By the voice of conscience.
2. That our works are alone acceptable to God, if done through the grace and impulsion of the Spirit.

*Into the wilderness.* Here note—
1. That Christ went into the wilderness to make expiation in His body for our excesses; to endure poverty for our luxury, want for our abundance.
2. That Christ went into the wilderness immediately after baptism, to teach us that, by baptism, we are called to renounce the world, and to lead a life of mortification.
3. That Christ sets us an example of retirement from the world and its turmoil, at seasons.
4. That Christ, by His example, has sanctioned and sanctified the life of the eremite.

*To be tempted of the devil.* Here note—
1. That, in order to be able to resist the devil, we must be furnished with the Holy Spirit.

2. That God suffers us to be tempted for wise purposes—
   *a.* To bring out our hidden virtues; thus He brought out the virtue of faith in Abraham by tempting him to slay his son, and the virtue of patience in Job by suffering him to be afflicted with loss of substance, health, and friends.
   β. To keep us vigilant. (1 Pet. v. 8.)
   γ. To reward us finally for our merit in resisting temptation. (James i. 12.)

3. A. The word 'to tempt' has three significations in Holy Scripture. It signifies—
   *a.* To bring out hidden graces; and thus is used of God tempting us. (Gen. xxii. 1.)
   β. To lead into sin; and thus is used of the devil tempting us. (1 Cor. vii. 5.)
   γ. To provoke to anger; and thus is used of our tempting God. (Ps. xcv. 9. Acts v. 9. Heb. i. 12.)

  B. God tempts us in Lent, drawing out of us a proof—
   *a.* Whether we love ourselves better than Him.
   β. Whether we love our souls better than our bodies.
   γ. Whether we love our present corruptible bodies better than our future incorruptible bodies.
   δ. Whether we love to obey the Church better than to follow our own wills.

4. Christ endured temptation from the devil—
   a. That He might prove the force of every temptation by which we are assailed.
   β. That He might show us how to meet temptation.
   γ. That He might break the force of temptation.
   δ. That He might teach us to expect temptation.

*And when He had fasted forty days and forty nights.*

Note that Christ fasted, though there was no need for Him to mortify His body, in that His body was free from sin.

*Forty days and forty nights.* Here note—
1. That forty represents the law as amplified by the Gospel, 10 × 4.
   a. Forty days did the rain descend to flood the world. (Gen. vii. 4.)
   β. Forty days were corpses dressed with aromatic herbs before consigning them to the grave. (Gen. l. 3.)
   γ. Forty years did Israel wander in the wilderness.
   δ. Forty days did Moses spend, on two occasions, in the mount. (Exod. xxiv. 18; xxxiv. 28.)
   ε. Forty days did Goliath defy the armies of the living God. (1 Sam. xvii. 16.)
   ζ. Forty days did Ezekiel bear the iniquities of the children of Israel. (Ezek. iv. 6.)

η. Forty days did Elijah fast in the desert. (1 Kings xix. 8.)

θ. Forty days did Nineveh afflict itself in sackcloth and ashes. (Jonah iii. 4.)

ι. Forty days was Christ with His Apostles after the resurrection. (Acts i. 3.)

2. We keep forty days of Lenten fast—

α. That we may represent in the Christian year the fasting of our Lord, as we also represent His birth, His death, His resurrection, and His ascension.

β. That we may appease God's wrath against us; making satisfaction to the best of our power for our fallings short during the rest of the year.

γ. That we may practise and test our strength, so as to be able to exert it when temptation arises.

δ. That we may fulfil Christ's words, *When the Bridegroom is taken away, then shall ye fast in those days.*

ε. That we may worthily prepare for the great solemnity of Easter, suffering with Christ that we may also be glorified together.

3. The advantages of fasting are,—

α. It keeps the body under, and brings it into subjection; giving us the habit of obtaining a mastery over our appetites.

β. It disposes the soul for prayer, and the mind for meditation.

γ. It makes reparation for past offences. (Jonah iii. 5—10.)

δ. It is meritorious, being one of those three works of which Christ has said that it shall be openly rewarded. (Matt. vi. 18.)

*And when the tempter came to Him, he said.* Here note—

I. a. The devil is called tempter, as one who builds is called a builder, and one who paints is called a painter: from the work upon which he is constantly engaged.

β. The devil probably came in human form, as angels when appearing to men assumed human forms. It seems likely that Satan had not fathomed that mystery, which angels desired to look into, the mystery of the Incarnation, and that he did not know that Christ was Incarnate God: yet was he filled with vague alarm.

γ. Christ's temptations came from without; they could not proceed from within, as His nature was sinless.

II. We also learn—

1. That solitude is not freedom from temptation, but rather a time for it.

2. That Satan expends the whole force of temptation on those who are leading a life of high vocation.

3. That Satan suits his temptation to the occasion.

4. That if Christ endured temptation, no man must expect to escape it.
5. That if Christ suffered Satan to approach Him with temptation, He will not reject us drawing nigh unto Him in prayer.
6. That temptations come to us in disguise: the evil one seldom presenting himself to us in his naked deformity.

*If Thou art the Son of God.* Here note—

Satan had heard the voice from Heaven, proclaiming Christ to be the beloved Son of God; but he may have considered Him as a son in some sense as Adam, who was called a son of God. That he could have grasped the mystery of the hypostatic union is impossible. Sin produces blindness, and Satan could not have seen and comprehended God's purposes. Had he believed Christ to be very and eternal God, it is inconceivable that he should have thought it possible to tempt Him into sin, unless the eyes of his understanding were so obscured by his pride that he had lost belief in all good, that he actually could imagine the Godhead to be peccable, just as a prostitute disbelieves in the purity of the most spotless virgin.

*If Thou art.* Note—

I. That Satan tempts even by that little word *if;* implying a doubt whether God had meant what He said when the voice came from

Heaven; by this word *if* Satan endeavoured to drive Him into—

a. The sin of pride: by causing Him to perform a miracle, so as to prove Himself to be the Son of God, and thus to dispel the doubt of the querist.

β. The sin of doubt: by causing Him to question the declaration from Heaven; for Satan's *if* implied that God, had He meant that Christ were His Son, would not have left Him to starve.

II. That it does not behove us to question the dealings of God's providence, though He suffer us to want, nor if He refuse to hear our petitions. Perhaps we ask for what is wrong, unsafe, or contrary to His will.

*Command that these stones be made bread.* Here note—

1. God wills to draw us from temporal things to things spiritual, but the devil obtrudes carnal matters, to draw us from spiritual things to things temporal.

2. The temptation of Christ bears some analogy to that of our first parents. Eve was tempted by the sight of the fruit which was good for food, Christ by the cravings of natural hunger.

3. Satan tempts us through our need for the necessaries of life. Thus some steal, others cheat, others live unchaste lives, under the excuse that they do it for a livelihood.

4. If Christ by a word can change stones into bread,

can He not change bread into His true and sacred Flesh?

5. Satan tempts Christ to make more than was necessary, *these stones,* so that He might fall into the sin of gluttony.

6. Satan tempts Christ to a false humility, by urging Him to make bread, the plainest food of the poor, instead of costly viands.

7. Satan never offers what can satisfy. The prodigal son was given but the husks, and here Satan presents nought but stones.

8. Christ left Satan still in doubt as to whether He were the Son of God or not: teaching us pious reserve on the subject of spiritual favours.

*And He answered and said, It is written, Man shall not live by bread alone, but by every word that proceedeth out of the mouth of God.* Here note—

1. Christ implies that God's power is not limited to the means prescribed by Satan. God can satisfy His own sons in ways of His own devising.

2. Christ passes over the challenge, *If Thou art the Son of God,* teaching us that our spiritual privileges are not to be proclaimed, but rather concealed, that pearls are not to be cast before swine, nor the children's bread to be given to dogs.

3. Christ's words imply the full inspiration of Scripture: He says, that man shall live by *every word;* not by the general sense.

4. Christ's words are prophetic: they indicate the fact that He Himself was to be the true food of man, He being the Word of God, He to be present as man's spiritual food and sustenance in the Blessed Sacrament of the Altar, until the end of time.
5. Christ answered in the words of Scripture, teaching us that in Scripture, as in an armoury, are the weapons of our spiritual warfare. The sword of the Spirit is the Word of God.

*Then the devil taketh Him up into the holy city, and setteth Him on a pinnacle of the temple, and saith unto Him.* Here note—

1. In the first temptation we have Satan coming to our Blessed Lord as a man moved with compassion for His famished condition. In the second, he appears as an angel of light, bearing Him to the holy city, as the angel bore Habakkuk to Babylon, and the Spirit of the Lord caught away Philip to Azotus. In the third, he presents himself as a god demanding worship.
2. Christ's great love is noticeable here, in suffering Himself to be borne hither and thither, whithersoever the tempter listed. So did He afterwards suffer Himself to be dragged by the wicked Jews from the judgment hall to Gabbatha and to Calvary. So too now does He suffer His sacred body to be in the hands and mouths of unworthy priests and lay communi-

cants, and to be offered in the meanest chapel, and to be carried to the filthiest hovel of the sick.
3. Temptation to spiritual pride is severe to those who are leading a high spiritual life; temptation to pride is common to all who are placed in high positions, whether in Church or State.
4. We must not be scandalized at the manner in which Episcopal appointments are made, whether by intrigue, or by State interference; Christ was exalted to a pinnacle of the temple by the devil, and many a holy man may be elevated to the dignity of the Episcopacy by the vilest of means.

*Holy city*, so called because—
1. In it was the temple of God.
2. Christ was present in the city to sanctify it.
3. It was a shadow of the Heavenly Jerusalem.

*If Thou be the Son of God, cast Thyself down.* Note—
This temptation followed the other as though deduced from it. Satan implied, "You have done well in showing your reliance on God; perfect your reliance, prove how complete it is." Observe also that—
1. Christ's temptation is not only to spiritual pride, but also to vain-glory, in that the prospect was before Him of being seen by men, supported by angelic hands, and thus of establishing His position as a prophet, at the outstart of His ministry.

2. Satan not only makes use of our natural wants, but even of our virtues, as means of temptation; urging us to carry them to excess. But virtue consists in moderation, in neither doing too much nor too little. Thus liberality lies between avarice and prodigality, and compunction is the mean betwixt assurance and despair.

3. Satan has no power to cast us down without the consent of our own free wills. He may urge to fall, but he cannot compel man to fall.

4. Satan endeavours to cast down to earth, whilst Christ is ever striving to draw man from earth, to lead man *to seek those things which are above.* (Col. iii. 2.)

5. We are guilty of casting ourselves down from the pinnacle upon which we are placed, whenever —

    *a.* We presumptuously neglect the natural means of support with which God has supplied us.

    *β.* We deliberately fall into sin, with the purpose of expiating it afterwards by confession.

    *γ.* We undertake any unprofitable task. For a Christian should set before him nothing upon which to expend his time and energies but what is of utility.

    *δ.* We do evil that good may come.

*For it is written, He shall give His angels charge*

*concerning Thee: and in their hands they shall bear Thee up, lest at any time Thou dash Thy foot against a stone.*

I. Satan placed two dangers before our Lord: that of being dashed to pieces, and that of committing a sin.

To remove the fear of either committing the sin, or of exposing Himself to danger, Satan quotes Scripture. He does this on two grounds—

1. To exhibit himself in a favourable light, as though he were the angel of God sent to bear Christ up.
2. To remove the fear of injury, on the authority of Scripture promises.

II. Satan endeavours to remove the prospect of danger, so as to make the thought of committing the sin less alarming. For many are deterred from crime by fear of its consequences; and if the fear be removed, then they are ready to commit the sin.

Eve was prevented from disobeying God by the fear of the consequences (Gen. iii. 3); Satan removed the fear when he said, *Ye shall not surely die;* and then at once the woman fell. So when Satan removes the fear of death, as something doleful to think upon, when we are in health, we are ready enough to sin. Whereas fear is salutary; as says Scripture, *To fear the Lord is the beginning of wisdom.* Ecclus. i. 14. 16. Matt. iii. 7. Luke xii. 5. Examples of the fear of the Lord

deterring from sin in Gen. xxxix. 9. Hist. Susanna 23.
III. Satan quotes Scripture for his own vile purposes, to screen himself under the semblance of piety. We have a warning here against those renegade Catholic priests and monks who desert the Church and the authority of the Bishops, that they may give themselves up to heresy and to unclean living, sheltering themselves all the while under Scripture texts distorted to serve their own purposes.
IV. Satan garbles Scripture in quoting it.
   1. He distorts the sense. Christ needed not angelic hands to sustain Him, and therefore the passage is not applicable to Him, but refers to His people. (Acts i. 9. Heb. i. 3.)
   2. He omits passages which did not suit his purpose. The words are, *They shall keep Thee in all Thy ways*, i. e. in the ways of God's commandments, not in breaking those commands. He also omits, *Thou shalt go upon the lion and adder: the young lion and the dragon shalt Thou tread under Thy feet*, because those words referred to himself as overcome by Christ.
V. Note also how great is the dignity of the true servant of God, upon whom, by God's command, the angels wait. Hence we may learn:—
   1. Not to regard ourselves as of no value, for

we are so highly esteemed of God that He commissions His own ministers to attend on us.

2. To entrust ourselves altogether to their guidance, for they will keep us in perfect peace.

3. To lead such a life as will make the angels surround us, and be our constant attendants. As bees swarm about a bed of flowers, so will they gather around those who bloom with Christian graces. Thus, the Bride is spoken of as *terrible as an army with banners*, that army of the living God, the angelic hosts of *chariots and horses of fire* surrounding the faithful. Around the bed of Solomon were *threescore valiant men*. And angels are about our bed watching and protecting us.

*Jesus said unto him, Thou shalt not tempt the Lord thy God.* Note here that—

I. Christ does not enter into a long discussion with the devil, but at once silences him, knowing his obduracy. (Tit. iii. 10.) He teaches us thereby not to parley with diabolic suggestions, but at once to suppress them.

II. Christ answered in the words of Scripture, to show us how to meet the assaults of the evil one; not with weapons of our own devising, but with those taken from the armoury of God's Word.

III. Christ met and overcame Satan with his own

weapon. Thus did David slay Goliath with his own sword; thus was Haman hanged on his own gallows; thus did Christ triumph at the last over Satan by a tree, wherewith Satan had ruined man.

IV. We tempt the Lord our God, whenever—
1. Presumptuously we require Him to alter the course of nature on our behalf.
2. We rush needlessly into danger.
3. We thoughtlessly cast ourselves into prayer, without having prepared our minds as to what we shall ask. (Eccles. xviii. 23.)
4. We persevere in sin that grace may abound, postponing repentance, stopping our ears to the calls of God.
5. We tie God down to means, as the princes of Bethulia tempted God, when they said that they would give up the city in five days. (Judith viii. 11.)
6. We attempt to excogitate the meaning of Scripture, with regard to doctrine, for ourselves, without following the direction of our divinely-constituted and infallible guide, the Church.
7. We stifle the promptings of conscience.
8. We neglect the appointed means of grace for those of our own choosing.

*Again the devil taketh Him up into an exceeding high mountain, and showeth Him all the kingdoms of the world, and the glory of them;* and St. Luke adds, *in a moment of time.*

I. Whereas St. John was shown the kingdoms of the world become the kingdom of the Lord and of His Christ, in ecstatic vision, here in vision are the kingdoms of the world shown to Christ as bowing under the rule of Satan.

II. Note also, how that—

1. Satan exhibited all the kingdoms to tempt Christ, whilst to tempt us one jug of wine, one fair woman, one handful of gold, are deemed quite sufficient.

2. Satan showed the *glory* of the kingdoms of earth, but not their emptiness, their troubles, their fleetingness.

3. Satan spreads the net of ambition before those who are leading a life of high spirituality. Thus the Apostles, who had forsaken all for Christ, yet strove amongst themselves as to which of them should be the greatest. (Luke xxii. 24. 2 Kings xxiv. 2.)

4. Satan showed the glories of earth, not of Heaven, trying by this temptation also to withdraw Christ's mind from things above to things below.

5. Satan did not show the real kingdoms, but only a semblance of them. So he offers us, not those things which will satisfy, but things which have no substance. (James iv. 14.)

Whatsoever there is in this world of glory, of beauty, of majesty, is but the shadow of *good things to come.* Satan tries to urge us to clasp the shadow, that we may lose the substance.

6. Satan showed all *in a moment of time;* we learn thereby—

   α. That his temptations come upon us with great suddenness.

   β. That the things he offers us are fleeting and without stability. In this world nothing is enduring. (1 Cor. vii. 35.) If Satan gives us what we desire, he removes it from us speedily. (Ps. lxxvi. 5. Prov. xiii. 11.)

*And saith unto Him, All these things will I give Thee, if Thou wilt fall down and worship me.* Here note—

I. Satan no longer says, *If Thou be the Son of God,* for he is now presenting himself as God, and might therefore be supposed to know all things.

II. Note here also, that—

1. The devil's motive in tempting man is still his unconquered pride. Still does he desire to be equal with God. But one of the three things which God hateth is, *a poor man that is proud* (Ecclus. xxv. 2); and who is poorer than the devil, yet who more proud?

2. All sin leads to the worship of Satan, and the breach of the First Commandment. For sin is a turning from the obedience of God to the bondage of cor-

ruption, a leaving the kingdom of grace for the slavery of sin, an electing of eternal death in the realm of outer darkness in place of resurrection to eternal life in the kingdom of Christ. All sin leads to this, for—

α. Sin must inherit death and damnation.

β. Sins lead to infidelity. (Ps. xiv. 1. Prov. xviii. 3.)

γ. They make gods of mammon or the belly. (Tobit iii. 3. Phil. iii. 19. Eph. v. 5.)

3. Satan is like a merchant offering wares in exchange for souls; like the king of Sodom who said, *Give me the souls, and take the goods to thyself.* (Gen. xiv. 21, Vulg.) But *what shall it profit a man, if he shall gain the whole world and lose his own soul?*

4. Satan tells here three lies.

α. He claims the world and its kingdoms as his own, whereas they belong to God. *The whole world is Mine, and all that therein is.*

β. He says that he gives kingdoms to whom he will (St. Luke); whereas God says, *By Me kings reign.* (Prov. viii. 15. Dan. ii. 21. John xii. 31.)

γ. He says that he has power to bestow things, whereas he has no such power whatever.

5. Satan tempts Christ to fall down: and so—

α. His deceptions have all one object: the accomplishment of our fall.

β. No man can worship Satan, without falling first most grievously.

6. Satan begins with small temptations, and ends with great ones; begins with a matter of bread, and ends with an offer of kingdoms. This teaches us not to despise small temptations; they are the forerunners of greater ones, the *little foxes* which spoil *the vines*. (Cant. ii. 15.) Give an inch, and Satan will take an ell. St. Peter began his fall by mixing with bad company about a fire; he ended by denying his Master with oaths and curses.

*Then saith Jesus unto him, Get thee hence, Satan; for it is written, Thou shalt worship the Lord thy God, and Him only shalt thou serve.*

I. Hitherto Christ has answered with gentleness, as the shafts of the devil were aimed simply at Himself as man; but now that Satan casts the arrow of blasphemy against God, He is kindled with zeal: thereby teaching us to bear our own injuries with meekness, but to resent with the flame of indignation any affront offered to the majesty of God. So Christ endured patiently being called a gluttonous man and a winebibber, but He was fired with zeal when He saw His Father's house made a house of merchandise.

II. Christ said not, *Get thee behind Me, Satan;* but, *Get thee hence, Satan:* for to Satan there was left no place for repentance, whilst to Peter, all that was needed was a following of Jesus in His humiliations and sufferings.

III. The weapons wielded by Christ in His temptation, were, pure trust in God, the Word of God, and hatred of the devil.

IV. It is of advantage that when we are tempted, we should recognize the tempter through his disguise. Temptation loses half its power when it is recognized as a temptation. When Christ showed Satan that He knew him, at once Satan took to flight. (1 Cor. xi. 14. 2 Cor. ii. 11. 1 John iii. 4.)

V. Christ made no allusion to Satan's offer, but passed at once to the condition, to show us that we should not suffer his allurements to find the smallest lodgment in our minds.

VI. Christ made use of the words, *Thou shalt worship the Lord thy God*, instead of *Thou shalt fear the Lord thy God*, Deut. vi. 13, from which He quoted, to show that in Him we have passed from the bondage of fear to the liberty of love, from the fear of servants to the reverence of children, that we have come to the *perfect love* of the New Covenant, which *casteth out fear* of the Old Law.

VII. Christ teaches us that God demands *worship* and bodily reverence, that reverence of falling down on the knee which Satan asked for himself.

VIII. Christ says not only, *Thou shalt worship the Lord thy God*, but also, *Him only shalt thou serve:* to teach us that bodily and spiritual worship is insufficient, unless it is followed by obedient service; that acts of devotion must go hand in hand with observance of the commandments.

*Then the devil leaveth Him, and behold angels came and ministered unto Him.*

*Leaveth Him*, St. Luke adds, *for a season*; for Satan returned to Him with provocations throughout His life, and finally afflicted Him on the cross. It was of his coming to Him then that Christ spoke, when He said, *The Prince of this world cometh, and hath nothing in Me.* (John xiv. 30.) It was then on the cross that Christ endured the last assaults of Satan: then, when He made that offering of a sweet-smelling savour, which, *when the evil spirit had smelled, he fled into the uttermost parts of Egypt, and the angel bound him.* (Tobit viii. 3.)

Note here likewise that—

The devil leaveth Christ: thus does he also leave us, after having tempted us,—

α. In the hopes of returning with seven other spirits to take up a permanent abode in man's heart, if found empty of the love of Jesus.

β. That he may plot some new form of temptation; retiring to gather strength. We must use this time of freedom for recruiting our forces and collecting additional arms of defence.

γ. That he may throw us off our guard, luring us into false security and spiritual sloth:—tempting us by his very absence.

*Angels came and ministered unto Him*, when the temptation was ended. In like manner will angels minister to us if we successfully resist.

Observe also that—

I. This brings great consolation to the religious, who have pledged themselves to the angelic life of poverty, chastity, and obedience.
   1. Christ overcame the temptation of the flesh when He rejected the offered stones.
   2. Christ overcame the temptation to disobedience and self-glorification when He remained on the pinnacle of the temple instead of showing a form of *will-worship* and *voluntary humility* by casting Himself down. And so should religious occupy any position to which their superior appoints them without seeking to desert it.
   3. Christ overcame the temptation to avarice when He rejected the offered kingdoms of the world: electing rather, poverty.

II. Angelic consolation follows retirement: the angels ministered to Christ in the wilderness. It follows victory over temptation: the angels ministered to Christ when the temptation was ended.

III. Conflict with Satan does not lead to conquest:

Christ took no spoils by His triumph. It is rather the victory of successful defence, of having *lost* nothing in the struggle, not of having gained aught.

Now I ask any candid person whether this is not a marvellous sermon, abounding in thought, overflowing with suggestions? Having read it, will he take up Scott, or Matthew Henry, or D'Oyly and Mant, and see what those luminaries have to say on the passage of Scripture thus wrought out by the Jesuit preacher?

I have not the least doubt as to the opinion he will form on the contrast.

We may truly say of the majority of Protestant commentators, that—*Their minds are blinded: for until this day remaineth the veil—upon their heart—in the reading of the Old*, or *New, Testament*. This is more applicable, of course, to foreign reformed theologians—if I may use the term theologian of those who are ignorant of the first principles of theology—than to our own divines. The English Church has always studied the Fathers, and has loved them; there is no great gulf fixed between us and the Mediævals, as there is between the Church and Protestant sectaries, and gleams of patristic light are reflected in the pages of our great divines. But there are commentators among us, such as Scott, who, scorning the master-expositors of early and Mediæval days, go to the study of God's Word with the veil of their self-sufficiency on their hearts, and become hopelessly involved in heresy.

Scott affords us a melancholy example of a mistaken

vocation. A commentator on Holy Scripture should be a man of profound theological learning, and of great intellectual power. Scott, a most amiable and pious clergyman, was neither a well-read man, nor were his abilities at all above par. His voluminous Commentary is accordingly, though overflowing with pious sentiment, of small theological value.

Protestant clergy commenting on Scripture, amidst the bustle of their ministerial avocations and their connubial distractions, without referring to the great works of early and Mediæval theologians, whose whole lives were spent in prayer and Scriptural studies, stand the chance of blundering as grossly as would a farm labourer if he undertook to excogitate, for himself, a system of astronomy, without reference to any treatises on the science already existing, or qualifying himself for the study, by a mastery of the rule of three, but regarded with unmitigated contempt all the discoveries made by those who have spent their lives in the exclusive study of the stars, and rejected as useless all the appliances of art invented to facilitate this investigation.

# INDEX.

ABSURD sermons, 18—21. 70—73
Alberti, Leander, 19
Anecdotes
  of F. de Neuilly, 11
  told by Balzac, 12
  of Cambridge preacher, 43, 44
  of Franciscan preacher, 44
  of Chaussemer, 45
  of the Père Seraphim, 45
  of Felix trembling, 47, 48
  of a long sermon, 55
  of Jerome de Narni, 57
  of St. John Capistran, 57
  of a public confession, 57
  of a usurer, 58
  of the Devil preaching, 81
  of Hannibal, 143

Bequest to Apollo, 13
Birds, 29—31
Bon-mots, 15, 16

Catholic preachers, 23—25
Classical allusions, 13, 14. 192
Commentators, 39. 235, 236
Conclusions, 56

D'Oyly and Mant, 40. 235

Effects produced by sermons, 56—58
Exordium, 13. 45—47

Flowers, 31—33
Friar-preachers, 17

Gratian de Drusac, 79

Henry IV., 16
Horæ Homileticæ, 54

James I., 43

Lapide, Cornelius à, 156
Lapide, Joannes de, 83
Lengthy sermon, 55
Louis XIV., 45
Love of nature, 28—33

Mademoiselle d'Entragues, 16
Marginal notes, 12
Mariolatry, 27. 84
Mystical interpretations, 37—43. 85. 124. 141. 187

Natural history, 84. 88. 94-97. 139
Nature, love of, 28—33

Oblates, 161
Open-air sermons, 11. 17

Parker, Matthew, 9
Preachers,
  Adrien Mangotius, 59, 60
  Alfric, 10
  Ambrose, St., 8
  Andrew of Crete, St., 10
  André, le Père, 15
  Andrewes, Bp., 60
  Angé de Rouen, 19
  Antonio Vieyra, 60
  Athanasius, St., 7
  Augustine, St., 8
  Barlette, Gabriel, 16. 19, 20

Preachers (*continued*)
  Barzia, Joseph de, 27. 33. 134—154. 178
  Basil, St., 8
  Basil of Seleucia, 9
  Bede, the Venerable, 10
  Biel, Gabriel, 12. 61—68
  Borgia, Francis, 132
  Bourdaloue, 60
  Brydaine, Jacques, 45—47
  Cæsarius of Arles, St., 9
  Camus, Bp. of Belley, 14
  Capistran, St. John, 57
  Celles, Peter of, 43
  Chrysostom, St., 8
  Claude, 54
  Clement of Alexandria, St., 7
  Coster, Francis, 206—236
  Cyprian, St., 7, 8
  Damascene, St. John, 10
  Deza, Maximilian, 192—205
  Ephraem Syrus, St., 7
  Eucher, St., 9
  Faber, Matthias, 31. 49—54. 100—115
  Foulque de Neuilly, 11
  Geminiano, John, 53, 59. 145
  Gonthier, le Père, 16
  Granada, Louis of, 12
  Gregory the Great, St., 8
  Gregory Nazianzen, St., 8
  Guerin, le Père, 15
  Guevara, Antonio de, Bp. of Mondoneda, 56
  Harphius, Henry, 22. 158
  Harrone, le Père d', 60
  Hartung, Philip von, 29. 43. 116—133
  Helmesius, 26. 135
  Imbert, Father, 19
  Kempis, St. Thomas à, 22
  Königstein, 25
  Labat, 17
  Langton, Stephen, 43
  Latimer, Hugh, 60
  Leo, St., 8
  Macarii, the, 7
  Maillard, Oliver, 12, 13. 43. 70
  Marchant, Jacques, 40. 136. 155—176
  Meffreth, 70. 81—99

Preachers (*continued*)
  Menot, Michael, 21. 70
  Narni, Jerome de, 56
  Narni, Philip de, 12
  Neuilly, Foulque de, 11
  Origen, 7
  Osorius, John, 33, 34. 177—191
  Pantænus, St., 7
  Paoletti, 56
  Polygranus, 26
  Raulin, Jean, 69—80
  Salvian, 9
  Satan, 81
  Savonarola, 12
  Segneri, Paolo, 60. 134. 194
  Simeon, Mr., 54, 55
  Stella, 39, 40
  Turricremata, John, 22
  Valerian of Cemele, 9
  Venerable Bede, 10
  Vieyra, Antonio, 60
  Wulfstan of York, 10
Protestant preachers, 23—25
Proverbs, 114, 115

Relation between Nature and Revelation, 28, 29

Scott the commentator, 39. 235, 236
Scriptural illustrations, 34. 37
Sermons for,—
  First Sunday in Advent, 198—202
  Christmas Day, 14. 25
  St. John's Day, 153, 154
  Sunday after Christmas Day, 148—153
  Epiphany, 70—73
  First Sunday after Epiphany, 107—110. 119—125
  Sexagesima, 85—87
  Septuagesima, 64—68
  Ash-Wednesday, 194—198
  First Sunday in Lent, 213—236
  Fourth Sunday in Lent, 103—107
  Palm Sunday, 111—113
  Good Friday, 169—171
  Easter Day, 110, 111
  Easter Monday, 172, 173

Sermons for
  Low Sunday, 172, 173
  Easter Tide, 161—167
  Second Sunday after Easter, 126—131
  Ascension Day, 173—176. 186, 187
  Trinity Sunday, 181—185
  Second Sunday after Trinity, 88—93
  Fifth Sunday after Trinity, 140—144
  Sixth Sunday after Trinity, 144—147
  Fifteenth Sunday after Trinity, 29—33
  Eighteenth Sunday after Trinity, 137—140
  Twentieth Sunday after Trinity, 36, 37
  Feast of
    St. Andrew, 198—202
    The Purification of our Lady, 27, 28. 148—153
    The Annunciation, 28
    St. Peter, 14
    St. James, 189—191
    Transfiguration of our Lord, 49—54
    Nativity of our Lady, 28
    Name of Mary, 17
Similes, 22, 23. 34. 74. 113, 114. 139, 140. 142. 181—186
Subjects of sermons, 47—54
Sermon on
  Birds, 29. 31
  Danger of neglecting trifling faults, 137—140
  Example, bad, 148—153
  Elect, small number of, 36, 37
  Flowers, 31—33

Subjects of Sermons (*continued*)
Sermon on
  Heaven, 126—131
  Hell, 119—125
  Judgment, 198—205
  Resurrection of Lazarus, 186—189
  Shortness of life, 194—198
  Sower, parable of, 85—87
  Supper, parable of, 88—93
  Temptation, 213—235
  Uncertainty of our future condition, 153, 154
  Vanity of the work of sinners, 140—144
  Wounded Side, 169—171

Tales related in sermons, 75
  Beasts at penance, 75
  Toad and his son, 77
  Widow and her servant, 78
  Hermit and the way of safety, 79, 80
  Mice in the larder, 94, 95
  Poor Robin, 97, 98
  Hermit and the olive-tree, 98
  Priest and capon, 99
  Crab and oyster, 139
  Hannibal, 143
  Women and the clew of wool, 146
  Children and the child Jesus, 209
  Priest and the acolyte, 211
Texts, strange, 13. 43—45

Unction, 84

Viaud, Theophilus, 15
Violent denunciations,
Vitry, Jacques de, 11

THE END.

GILBERT AND RIVINGTON, PRINTERS, ST. JOHN'S SQUARE, LONDON.

October, 1865.

# A SELECT LIST OF WORKS

PUBLISHED BY

# MESSRS. RIVINGTON,

WATERLOO PLACE, LONDON;

HIGH STREET, OXFORD;

TRINITY STREET, CAMBRIDGE.

---

Adams's (Rev. W.) The Shadow of the Cross; an Allegory.
A New Edition, elegantly printed in crown 8vo., with Illustrations. 3s. 6d. in extra cloth, gilt edges.

The Shadow of the Cross; an Allegory.

The Distant Hills; an Allegory.

The Old Man's Home; an Allegorical Tale.

The King's Messengers; an Allegory.
These four works are printed uniformly in 18mo., with Engravings, price 9d. each in paper covers, or 1s. in limp cloth.

A Collected Edition of the Four Allegories, with Memoir and Portrait of the Author: elegantly printed in crown 8vo. 9s. in cloth, or 14s. in morocco.

An Illustrated Edition of the above Sacred Allegories, with numerous Engravings on Wood from Original Designs by C. W. Cope, R.A., J. C. Horsley, A.R.A., Samuel Palmer, Birket Foster, and George E. Hicks. Small 4to. 21s. in extra cloth, or 36s. in antique morocco.

Adams's (Rev. W.) The Warnings of the Holy Week; being a Course of Parochial Lectures for the Week before Easter, and the Easter Festivals. Fifth Edition. Small 8vo. 4s. 6d.

A

Ainger's (Rev. T.) Practical Sermons. Small 8vo. 6s.

Ainger's (Rev. T.) Last Sermons: with a Memoir of the Author prefixed. Small 8vo. 5s.

A Kempis, Of the Imitation of Christ. A carefully revised translation; elegantly printed by Whittingham, in small 8vo, price 5s. in antique cloth.

Alford's (Dean) Greek Testament; with a critically revised Text: a Digest of Various Readings: Marginal References to Verbal and Idiomatic Usage. Prolegomena: and a copious Critical and Exegetical Commentary in English. In 4 vols. 8vo. 5l. 2s.

*Or, separately,*

Vol. I.—The Four Gospels. Fifth Edition. 28s.
Vol. II.—Acts to II. Corinthians. Fifth Edition. 24s.
Vol. III.—Galatians to Philemon. Third Edition. 18s.
Vol. IV.—Hebrews to Revelation. Second Edition. 32s.
The Fourth Volume may still be had in Two Parts.

Alford's (Dean) New Testament for English Readers: containing the Authorized Version, with a revised English Text; Marginal References; and a Critical and Explanatory Commentary. In Two large Volumes, 8vo.

Already published,

Vol. I., Part 1, containing the first three Gospels, with a Map of the Journeyings of our Lord, 12s.
Vol. I., Part 2, containing St. John and the Acts, 10s. 6d.
Vol. II., Part 1, containing the Epistles of St. Paul, with a Map. 16s.

Alford's (Dean) Sermons on Christian Doctrine, preached in Canterbury Cathedral, on the Afternoons of the Sundays in the year 1861-62. Second Edition. Crown 8vo. 7s. 6d.

Alford's (Dean) Sermons preached at Quebec Chapel, 1854 to 1857. In Seven Volumes, small 8vo. 2l. 1s.

*Sold separately as follows:—*

Vols. I. and II. (A course for the Year.) Second Edition. 12s. 6d.
Vol. III. (On Practical Subjects.) 7s. 6d.
Vol. IV. (On Divine Love.) Third Edition. 5s.
Vol. V. (On Christian Practice.) Second Edition. 5s.
Vol. VI. (On the Person and Office of Christ.) 5s.
Vol. VII. (Concluding Series.) 6s.

Anderson's (Hon. Mrs.) Practical Religion exemplified, by Letters and Passages from the Life of the late Rev. Robert Anderson, of Brighton. Sixth Edition. Small 8vo. 4s.

Annual Register; a Review of Public Events at Home and Abroad, for the Years 1863 and 1864; being the First and Second Volumes of an improved Series. 8vo. 18s. each.

Arnold's School Series (see page 18).

Arnold's (Rev. T. K.) Sermons preached in a Country Village. Post 8vo. 5s. 6d.

Arnold's (Rev. Dr. T.) History of Rome, from the Earliest Period to the End of the Second Punic War. New Edition. 3 vols. 8vo. 36s.

Arnold's (Rev. Dr. T.) History of the later Roman Commonwealth, from the End of the Second Punic War to the Death of Julius Cæsar, with the Reign of Augustus, and a Life of Trajan. New Edition. 2 vols. 8vo. 24s.

Articles (The) of the Christian Faith, considered in reference to the Duties and Privileges of Christ's Church Militant here on Earth. Small 8vo. 3s. 6d.

Beaven's (Rev. Dr.) Questions on Scripture History. Fourth Edition, revised. 18mo. 2s.

Beaven's (Rev. Dr.) Help to Catechising; for the use of Clergymen, Schools, and Private Families. New Edition. 18mo. 2s.

Bethell's (Bishop) General View of the Doctrine of Regeneration in Baptism. Fifth Edition. 8vo. 9s.

Bickersteth's (Archdeacon) Questions illustrating the Thirty-nine Articles of the Church of England: with Proofs from Scripture and the Primitive Church. Fifth Edition. 12mo. 3s. 6d.

Bickersteth's (Archdeacon) Catechetical Exercises on the Apostles' Creed; chiefly drawn from the Exposition of Bishop Pearson. New Edition. 18mo. 2s.

Blunt's (Rev. J. H.) Directorium Pastorale: the Principles and Practice of Pastoral Work in the Church of England. Crown 8vo. 9s.

This work has been written with the object of providing for Theological students and the younger Clergy a Practical Manual on the subject of which it treats.

Contents:—Chap. I. The nature of the Pastoral Office.—Chap. II. The relation of the Pastor to God —Chap. III. The relation of the Pastor to his flock.—Chap. IV. The ministry of God's Word.—Chap. V. The ministry of the Sacraments, &c.—Chap. VI. The Visitation of the Sick.—Chap. VII. Pastoral converse.— Chap. VIII. Private Instruction.—Chap. IX. Schools.—Chap. X. Parochial lay co-operation.—Chap. XI Auxiliary Parochial Institutions.—Chap. XII. Parish Festivals.—Chap. XIII. Miscellaneous Responsibilities.

Blunt's (Rev. J. H) Household Theology; a Handbook of Religious Information respecting the Holy Bible, the Prayer Book, the Church, the Ministry, Divine Worship, the Creeds, &c., &c. Small 8vo. 6s.

Boyle's (W. R. A.) Inspiration of the Book of Daniel, and other portions of Sacred Scripture. With a correction of Profane, and an adjustment of Sacred Chronology. 8vo. 14s.

Bright's (Rev. W.) Faith and Life; Readings for the greater Holydays, and the Sundays from Advent to Trinity. Compiled from Ancient Writers. Small 8vo. 5s.

Brown's (Rev. G. J.) Lectures on the Gospel according to St. John, in the form of a Continuous Commentary. 2 vols. 8vo. 24s.

Browne's (Sir Thomas) Christian Morals. With a Life of the Author by Samuel Johnson. In small 8vo. with Portrait of Author, price 6s. handsomely printed on toned paper from antique type.

Burke.—A Complete Edition of the Works and Correspondence of the Right Hon. Edmund Burke. In 8 vols. 8vo. *With Portrait.* 4l. 4s.

    Contents :—1. Mr. Burke's Correspondence between the year 1744 and his Decease in 1797, first published from the original MSS. in 1844, edited by Earl Fitzwilliam and Sir Richard Bourke. The most interesting portion of the Letters of Mr. Burke to Dr. French Laurence is also included in it.

    2. The Works of Mr. Burke, as edited by his Literary Executors, and completed by the publication of the 15th and 16th Volumes, in 1826, under the Superintendence of the late Bishop of Rochester, Dr. Walker King.

Burke's (Edmund) Reflections on the Revolution in France, in 1790. New Edition, with a short Biographical Notice. 8vo. 4s. 6d.

Cambridge Year-Book and University Almanack for 1865. Edited by William White, Sub-Librarian of Trinity College. Crown 8vo. 2s. 6d. sewed; or, 3s. 6d. in cloth.

Caswall's (Rev. Dr.) Martyr of the Pongas. A Memoir of the Rev. Hamble James Leacock, first West-Indian Missionary to Western Africa. Small 8vo. With Portrait. 5s. 6d.

Chase's (Rev. D. P.) Translation of the Nicomachean Ethics of Aristotle; with an Introduction, a Marginal Analysis, and Explanatory Notes. Designed for the use of Students in the Universities. Second Edition, revised. Crown 8vo. 6s.

Christian's (The) Duty, from the Sacred Scriptures. In Two Parts. [*London : sold by C. Rivington, in St. Paul's Churchyard.* 1730.] New Edition. Edited by the Rev. Thomas Dale, M.A. Small 8vo. (1852.) 5s.

Clergy Charities.—List of Charities, General and Diocesan, for the Relief of the Clergy, their Widows and Families. Fifth Edition. Small 8vo. 3s.

Clissold's (Rev. H.) Lamps of the Church; or, Rays of
Faith, Hope, and Charity, from the Lives and Deaths of some Eminent
Christians of the Nineteenth Century. *New and cheaper Edition.* Crown
8vo., with five Portraits. 5s.

Codd's (Rev. A.) The Fifty-Third Chapter of Isaiah. A
Course of Lectures, delivered in Holy Week and on Easter Day, in the
Parish Church of Beaminster, Dorset. Small 8vo. 3s. 6d.

Cotterill's Selection of Psalms and Hymns for Public Worship. New and cheaper Editions. 32mo., 1s.; in 18mo. (large print),
1s. 6d. Also an Edition on fine paper, 2s. 6d.
\*\*\* A large allowance to Clergymen and Churchwardens.

Cox's (Miss) Hymns from the German; accompanied by the
German originals. Second Edition, elegantly printed in small 8vo. 5s.

Cox's (Rev. J. M.) The Church on the Rock: or, the Claims
and some Distinctive Doctrines of the Church of Rome considered, in Six
Lectures. Small 8vo. 3s.

Coxe's (Archdeacon) Plain Thoughts on Important Church
Subjects. Small 8vo. 3s.

Crosthwaite's (Rev. J. C.) Historical Passages and Characters in the Book of Daniel; Eight Lectures, delivered in 1852, at the
Lecture founded by the late Bernard Hyde, Esq. To which are added,
Four Discourses on Mutual Recognition in a Future State. 12mo.
7s. 6d.

Daily Service Hymnal. 12mo., 1s. 6d. 32mo., 6d.

Davys's (Bp. of Peterborough) Plain and Short History of
England for Children: in Letters from a Father to his Son. With Questions. Fourteenth and Cheaper Edition. 18mo. 1s. 6d.

Denton's (Rev. W.) Commentary, Practical and Exegetical,
on the Lord's Prayer. Small 8vo. 5s.

Elliott's (Rev. H. Venn) Sermons at Cambridge, 1850-54.
Crown 8vo. 7s.

Ellison's (Rev. H. J.) Way of Holiness in Married Life;
a Course of Sermons preached in Lent. Second Edition. Small 8vo.
2s. 6d. *In white cloth, antique style,* 3s. 6d.

Englishman's (The) Magazine of Literature, Religion, Science,
and Art. Vol. I., January to June, 1865. 8vo. 7s. 6d.

Espin's (Rev. T. E.) Critical Essays. Crown 8vo. 7s. 6d.
Contents:—Wesleyan Methodism—Essays and Reviews—Edward
Irving—Sunday—Bishop Wilson, of Sodor and Man—Bishop Wilson, of
Calcutta—Calvin.

Evans's (Rev. R. W.) Bishopric of Souls. Fourth Edition.
Small 8vo. 5s.

Evans's (Rev. R. W.) Ministry of the Body. Second Edition. Small 8vo. 6s. 6d.

Exton's (Rev. R. B.) Speculum Gregis; or, the Parochial Minister's Assistant in the Oversight of his Flock. With blank forms to be filled up at discretion. Seventh Edition. In pocket size. 4s. 6d. bound with clasp.

Fearon's (Rev. H.) Sermons on Public Subjects. Small 8vo. 3s. 6d.

Fulford's (Bp. of Montreal) Sermons, Addresses, and Statistics of the Diocese. 8vo. 5s.

Gilly's (Rev. Canon) Memoir of Felix Neff, Pastor of the High Alps; and of his Labours among the French Protestants of Dauphiné, a Remnant of the Primitive Christians of Gaul. Sixth Edition. Fcap. 5s. 6d.

Girdlestone's (Rev. Charles) Holy Bible, containing the Old and New Testaments; with a Commentary arranged in Short Lectures for the Daily Use of Families. New Edition, in 6 vols, 8vo. 3l. 3s.
    The Old Testament separately. 4 vols. 8vo. 42s.
    The New Testament. 2 vols. 8vo. 21s.

Goulburn's (Rev. Dr.) Thoughts on Personal Religion. Eighth Edition, revised and enlarged. Small 8vo. 6s. 6d.

Goulburn's (Rev. Dr.) Office of the Holy Communion in the Book of Common Prayer; a Series of Lectures delivered in the Church of St. John the Evangelist, Paddington. Third Edition. Small 8vo. 6s.

Goulburn's (Rev. Dr.) Sermons preached on Various Occasions during the last Twenty Years. Second Edition. 2 vols. small 8vo. 10s. 6d.

Goulburn's (Rev. Dr.) The Idle Word: Short Religious Essays upon the Gift of Speech, and its Employment in Conversation. Third Edition. Small 8vo. 3s.

Goulburn's (Rev. Dr.) Introduction to the Devotional Study of the Holy Scriptures. Seventh Edition. Small 8vo. 3s. 6d.

Goulburn's (Rev. Dr.) Family Prayers, arranged on the Liturgical Principle. Third Edition. Small 8vo. 3s.

Goulburn's (Rev. Dr.) Short Devotional Forms, compiled to meet the Exigencies of a Busy life. New Edition, elegantly printed in square 16mo. 1s. 6d.

Goulburn's (Rev. Dr.) Manual of Confirmation. Fifth Edition. 1s. 6d.

Gould's (Rev. S. B.) Post-Mediæval Preachers. Post 8vo. 7s.

Gray's (Rev. J. B.) Psalter, Festival and Ferial, pointed and adapted to the Gregorian Tones. Crown 8vo. 4s.

Greswell's (Rev. Edward) The Three Witnesses and the Threefold Cord; being the Testimony of the Natural Measures of Time, of the Primitive Civil Calendar, and of Antediluvian and Postdiluvian Tradition, on the Principal Questions of Fact in Sacred or Profane Antiquity. 8vo. 7s. 6d.

Greswell's (Rev. Edward) Objections to the Historical Character of the Pentateuch, in Part I. of Dr. Colenso's "Pentateuch and Book of Joshua," considered, and shown to be unfounded. 8vo. 5s.

Greswell's (Rev. Edward) Exposition of the Parables and of other Parts of the Gospels. 5 vols. (in 6 parts), 8vo. 3l. 12s.

Grotius de Veritate Religionis Christianæ. With English Notes and Illustrations, for the use of Students. By the Rev. J. E. Middleton, M.A., of Trinity College, Cambridge; Lecturer on Theology at St. Bees' College, Second Edition. 12mo. 6s.

Gurney's (Rev. J. H.) Sermons on the Acts of the Apostles. With a Preface by the Dean of Canterbury. Small 8vo. 7s.

Gurney's (Rev. J. H.) Sermons chiefly on Old Testament Histories, from Texts in the Sunday Lessons. Second Edition. 6s.

Gurney's (Rev. J. H.) Sermons on Texts from the Epistles and Gospels for Twenty Sundays. Second Edition. 6s.

Gurney's (Rev. J. H.) Miscellaneous Sermons. 6s.

Hale's (Archdeacon) Sick Man's Guide to Acts of Faith, Patience, Charity, and Repentance. Extracted from Bishop Taylor's Holy Dying. In large print. Second Edition. 8vo. 3s.

Hall's (Rev. W. J.) Psalms and Hymns adapted to the Services of the Church of England; with a Supplement of additional Hymns and Indices. In 8vo., 5s. 6d.—18mo., 3s.—24mo., 1s. 6d.—24mo., limp cloth, 1s. 3d.—32mo., 1s.—32mo., limp, 8d. (The Supplement may be had separately.)

*⁎* A Prospectus of the above, with Specimens of Type, and farther particulars, may be had of the Publishers.

Hall's Selection of Psalms and Hymns; with Accompanying Tunes, selected and arranged by John Foster, of Her Majesty's Chapels Royal. Crown 8vo., *limp cloth*, 2s. 6d. The Tunes only, 1s.

Hall's Selection. An Edition of the above Tunes for the Organ. Oblong 8vo. 7s. 6d.

Help and Comfort for the Sick Poor. By the Author of "Sickness: its Trials and Blessings." Fourth Edition, *in large print.* 1s., or 1s. 6d. in cloth.

Henley's (Hon. and Rev. R.) Sermons on the Beatitudes, preached at St. Mary's Church, Putney. Small 8vo. 3s.

Henley's (Hon. and Rev. R.) The Prayer of Prayers. Small 8vo. 4s. 6d.

Hessey's (Rev. Dr.) Biographies of the Kings of Judah: Twelve Lectures. Crown 8vo. 6s. 6d.

Heygate's (Rev. W. E.) Care of the Soul; or, Sermons on Points of Christian Prudence. 12mo. 5s. 6d.

Heygate's (Rev. W. E.) The Good Shepherd; or, Christ the Pattern, Priest, and Pastor. 18mo. 3s. 6d.

Hodgson's (Chr.) Instructions for the Use of Candidates for Holy Orders, and of the Parochial Clergy, as to Ordination, Licences, Induction, Pluralities, Residence, &c. &c.; with Acts of Parliament relating to the above, and Forms to be used. Eighth Edition, revised and corrected. 8vo. 12s.

Holden's (Rev. Geo.) Ordinance of Preaching investigated. Small 8vo. 3s. 6d.

Holden's (Rev. Geo.) Christian Expositor; or, Practical Guide to the Study of the New Testament. Intended for the use of General Readers. Second Edition. 12mo. 12s.

Hook's (Dean) Book of Family Prayer. Seventh Edition, revised and enlarged. 18mo. 2s.

Hook's (Dean) Private Prayers. Fifth Edition. 18mo. 2s.

Hook's (Dean) Dictionary of Ecclesiastical Biography. 8 vols. 12mo. 2l. 11s.

Hours (The) of the Passion; with Devotional Forms for Private and Household Use. 12mo. 5s. in limp cloth, or 6s. in cloth, red edges.

Hulton's (Rev. C. G.) Catechetical Help to Bishop Butler's Analogy. Third Edition. Post 8vo. 4s. 6d.

Hymns and Poems for the Sick and Suffering; in connexion with the Service for the Visitation of the Sick. Selected from various Authors. Edited by the Rev. T. V. Fosbery, M.A., Vicar of St. Giles's, Reading. Sixth Edition. 5s. 6d. *in cloth,* or 9s. 6d. *in morocco.*

Jackson's (Bp. of Lincoln) Six Sermons on the Christian Character; preached in Lent. Seventh Edition. Small 8vo. 3s. 6d.

James's (Rev. Dr.) Comment upon the Collects appointed to be used in the Church of England on Sundays and Holydays throughout the Year. Fifteenth Edition. 12mo. 5s.

James's (Rev. Dr.) Christian Watchfulness in the Prospect of Sickness, Mourning, and Death. Eighth Edition. 12mo. 6s.
Cheap Editions of these two works may be had, price 3s. each.

James's (Rev. Dr.) Evangelical Life, as seen in the Example of our Lord Jesus Christ. Second Edition. 12mo. 7s. 6d.

James's (Rev. Dr.) Devotional Comment on the Morning and Evening Services in the Book of Common Prayer, in a Series of Plain Lectures. Second Edition. In 2 vols. 12mo. 10s. 6d.

Inman's (Rev. Professor) Treatise on Navigation and Nautical Astronomy, for the Use of British Seamen. Thirteenth Edition, edited by the Rev. J. W. Inman. Royal 8vo. 7s.

Inman's (Rev. Professor) Nautical Tables for the Use of British Seamen. New Edition, edited by the Rev. J. W. Inman. Royal 8vo. 14s.     Or, with a new Table of Latitudes and Longitudes, 16s.

Jones's (Rev. Harry) Life in the World: Sermons at St. Luke's, Berwick Street. Small 8vo. 5s.

Kaye's (Bishop) Account of the Writings and Opinions of Justin Martyr. Third Edition. 8vo. 7s. 6d.

Kaye's (Bishop) Ecclesiastical History of the Second and Third Centuries, Illustrated from the Writings of Tertullian. Third Edition. 8vo. 13s.

Kaye's (Bishop) Account of the Writings and Opinions of Clement of Alexandria. 8vo. 12s.

Kaye's (Bishop) Account of the Council of Nicæa, in connexion with the Life of Athanasius. 8vo. 8s.

Kennaway's (Rev. C. E.) Consolatio; or, Comfort for the Afflicted. Selected from various Authors. With a Preface by the Bishop of Oxford. Eleventh Edition. Small 8vo. 4s. 6d.

Knowles's (Rev. E. H.) Notes on the Epistle to the Hebrews, with Analysis and Brief Paraphrase; for Theological Students. Crown 8vo. 6s. 6d.

Lee's (Archdeacon) Eight Discourses on the Inspiration of Holy Scripture. Fourth Edition. 8vo. 15s.

Lee's (Rev. F. G.) The Words from the Cross: Seven Sermons for Lent and Passion-tide. Second Edition. Small 8vo. 2s. 6d.

Lewis's (Rev. W. S.) Threshold of Revelation; or, Some Inquiry into the Province and True Character of the First Chapter of Genesis. Crown 8vo. 6s.

London Diocese Book for 1865 : containing an account of the
 See and its Bishops; of St. Paul's Cathedral, Westminster Abbey, and
 the Chapels Royal; of the Rural Deaneries, Foreign Chaplaincies, &c.
 By John Hassard, Private Secretary to the Bishop of London. Second
 Edition. Crown 8vo. 2s. 6d.

McCaul's (Rev. Dr.) Examination of Bp. Colenso's Difficulties with regard to the Pentateuch; and some Reasons for believing in
 its Authenticity and Divine Origin. Third Library Edition. Crown
 8vo. 5s.

McCaul's (Rev. Dr.) Examination of Bp. Colenso's Difficulties with regard to the Pentateuch. Part II. Crown 8vo. 2s.

Mackenzie's (Rev. H.) Ordination Lectures, delivered in
 Riseholme Palace Chapel, during Ember Weeks. Small 8vo. 3s.
  Contents:—Pastoral Government — Educational Work — Self-government in the Pastor—Missions and their Reflex Results—Dissent—Public
 Teaching—Sunday Schools—Doctrinal Controversy—Secular Aids.

Mansel's (Rev. Professor) Artis Logicæ Rudimenta, from
 the Text of Aldrich; with Notes and Marginal References. Fourth
 Edition, corrected and enlarged. 8vo. 10s. 6d.

Mansel's (Rev. Professor) Prolegomena Logica; an Inquiry
 into the Psychological Character of Logical Processes. Second Edition.
 8vo. 10s. 6d.

Mant's (Bishop) Book of Common Prayer and Administration of the Sacraments, with copious Notes, Practical and Historical,
 from approved Writers of the Church of England; including the Canons
 and Constitutions of the Church. New Edition. In one volume, super-
 royal 8vo. 24s.

Mant's (Bishop) Happiness of the Blessed considered as to
 the Particulars of their State; their Recognition of each other in that
 State; and its Difference of Degrees. Seventh Edition. 12mo. 4s.

Margaret Stourton; or, a Year of Governess Life. Elegantly printed in small 8vo. Price 5s.

Marriott's (Rev. Wharton B.) Adelphi of Terence, with
 English Notes. Small 8vo. 3s.

Marsh's (Bishop) Comparative View of the Churches of
 England and Rome: with an Appendix on Church Authority, the Character of Schism, and the Rock on which our Saviour declared that He
 would build His Church. Third Edition. Small 8vo. 6s.

Massingberd's (Rev. F. C.) Lectures on the Prayer-Book.
 Small 8vo. 3s. 6d.

Mayd's (Rev. W.) Sunday Evening; or, a Short and Plain
 Exposition of the Gospel for every Sunday in the Year. Crown 8vo.
 5s.

Medd's (Rev. P. G.) Household Prayer; with Morning and Evening Readings for a Month. Small 8vo. 4s. 6d.

Melvill's (Rev. H.) Sermons. Vol. I., Sixth Edition. Vol. II., Fourth Edition. 10s. 6d. each.

Melvill's (Rev. H.) Sermons on some of the less prominent Facts and References in Sacred Story. Second Series. 8vo. 10s. 6d.

Melvill's (Rev. H.) Selection from the Lectures delivered at St. Margaret's, Lothbury, on the Tuesday Mornings in the Years 1850, 1851, 1852. Small 8vo. 6s.

Middleton's (Bp.) Doctrine of the Greek Article applied to the Criticism and Illustration of the New Testament. With Prefatory Observations and Notes, by Hugh James Rose, B.D., late Principal of King's College, London. New Edition. 8vo. 12s.

Mill's (Rev. Dr.) Analysis of Bishop Pearson on the Creed. Third Edition. 8vo. 5s.

Miller's (Rev. J. K.) Parochial Sermons. Small 8vo. 4s. 6d.

Missing Doctrine (The) in Popular Preaching. Small 8vo. 5s.

Monsell's (Rev. Dr.) Parish Musings; or, Devotional Poems. Eighth Edition, elegantly printed on toned paper. Small 8vo. 2s. 6d.

Also, a CHEAP EDITION, price 1s. sewed, or 1s. 6d. in limp cloth.

Moore's (Rev. Daniel) The Age and the Gospel; Four Sermons preached before the University of Cambridge, at the Hulsean Lecture, 1864. Crown 8vo. 5s.

Moreton's (Rev. Julian) Life and Work in Newfoundland: Reminiscences of Thirteen Years spent there. Crown 8vo., *with a Map and four Illustrations*. 5s. 6d.

Mozley's (Rev. J. B.) Review of the Baptismal Controversy. 8vo. 9s. 6d.

Nixon's (Bishop) Lectures, Historical, Doctrinal, and Practical, on the Catechism of the Church of England. Sixth Edition. 8vo. 18s.

Notes on Wild Flowers. By a Lady. Small 8vo. 9s.

Old Man's (The) Rambles. Sixth and cheaper Edition. 18mo. 3s. 6d.

Parkinson's (Canon) Old Church Clock. Fourth Edition. Small 8vo. 4s. 6d.

Parry's (Mrs.) Young Christian's Sunday Evening; or, Conversations on Scripture History. In 3 vols. small 8vo. Sold separately:
> First Series: on the Old Testament. Fourth Edition. 6s. 6d.
> Second Series: on the Gospels. Third Edition. 7s.
> Third Series: on the Acts. Second Edition. 4s. 6d.

Parry's (Rev. E. St. John) School Sermons preached at Leamington College. Small 8vo. 4s. 6d.

Peile's (Rev. Dr.) Annotations on the Apostolical Epistles. New Edition. 4 vols. 8vo. 42s.

Pepys's (Lady C.) Quiet Moments: a Four Weeks' Course of Thoughts and Meditations before Evening Prayer and at Sunset. Fourth Edition. Small 8vo. 3s. 6d.

Pepys's (Lady C.) Morning Notes of Praise: a Companion Volume. Second Edition. 3s. 6d.

Pepys's (Lady C.) Thoughts for the Hurried and Hard-working. Second Edition, in large print, price 1s. sewed, or 1s. 6d. in limp cloth.

Physical Science compared with the Second Beast of the Revelations. Small 8vo. 3s. 6d.

Pigou's (Rev. Francis) Faith and Practice; Sermons at St. Philip's, Regent Street. Small 8vo. 6s.

Pinder's (Rev. Canon) Sermons on the Book of Common Prayer and Administration of the Sacraments. To which are now added, Several Sermons on the Feasts and Fasts of the Church, preached in the Cathedral Church of Wells. Third Edition. 12mo. 7s.

Pinder's (Rev. Canon) Sermons on the Holy Days observed in the Church of England throughout the Year. Second Edition. 12mo. 6s. 6d.

Pinder's (Rev. Canon) Meditations and Prayers on the Ordination Service for Deacons. Small 8vo. 3s. 6d.

Pinder's (Rev. Canon) Meditations and Prayers on the Ordination Service for Priests. Small 8vo. 3s. 6d.

Plain Sermons. By Contributors to the "Tracts for the Times." In 10 vols. 8vo., 6s. 6d. each. (Sold separately.)
> This Series contains 347 original Sermons of moderate length, written in simple language, and in an earnest and impressive style, forming a copious body of practical Theology, in accordance with the Doctrines of the Church of England. They are particularly suited for family reading. The last Volume contains a general Index of Subjects, and a Table of the Sermons adapted to the various Seasons of the Christian Year.

Prayers for the Sick and Dying. By the Author of "Sickness, its Trials and Blessings." Fourth Edition. Small 8vo. 2s. 6d.

Prichard's (Rev. C. E.) Commentary on Ephesians, Philippians, and Colossians, for English Readers. Crown 8vo. 4s. 6d.

Priest (The) to the Altar; or, Aids to the Devout Celebration of Holy Communion, chiefly after the Ancient English Use of Sarum. 8vo. 7s. 6d.

Public Schools (The) Calendar for 1865. Edited by a Graduate of the University of Oxford. Small 8vo. 6s.

*₊* This Work is intended to furnish Annually an account of the Foundations and Endowments of the Schools; of the Course of Study and Discipline; Scholarships and Exhibitions; Fees and other Expenses; School Prizes and University Honours; Recreations and Vacations; Religious Instruction; and other useful information.

Pusey's (Rev. Dr.) Commentary on the Minor Prophets: with Introductions to the several Books. In 4to.

Parts I., II., III., price 5s. each, are already published.

Pusey's (Rev. Dr.) Daniel the Prophet; Nine Lectures delivered in the Divinity School. Third Thousand. 8vo. 12s.

Pusey's (Rev. Dr.) Letter to Rev. J. Keble on the Restoration of Unity in the Church. 8vo. 7s. 6d.

Reminiscences by a Clergyman's Wife. Edited by the Dean of Canterbury. Second Edition. Crown 8vo. 3s. 6d.

Sargent's (J. Y.) Outlines of Norwegian Grammar, with Exercises. Small 8vo. 3s.

Schmitz's (Dr. L.) Manual of Ancient History, from the Remotest Times to the Overthrow of the Western Empire, A.D. 476. Third Edition. Crown 8vo. 7s. 6d.

This Work, for the convenience of Schools, may be had in Two Parts, sold separately, viz.:—

Vol. I., containing, besides the History of India and the other Asiatic Nations, a complete History of Greece. 4s.

Vol. II., containing a complete History of Rome. 4s.

Schmitz's (Dr. L.) Manual of Ancient Geography. Crown 8vo. 6s.

Schmitz's (Dr. L.) History of the Middle Ages, from the Downfall of the Western Empire, A.D. 476, to the Crusades, A.D. 1096. Crown 8vo. 7s. 6d.

Scripture Record of the Life and Times of Samuel the Prophet. By the Author of "Scripture Record of the Blessed Virgin." Small 8vo. 3s.

Seymour's (Rev. R.) and Mackarness's (Rev. J. F.) Eighteen
Years of a Clerical Meeting: being the Minutes of the Alcester Clerical
Association, from 1842 to 1860; with a Preface on the Revival of Ruri-
decanal Chapters. Crown 8vo. 6s. 6d.

Sickness, its Trials and Blessings. Seventh Edition. Small
8vo. 3s. 6d. Also, a cheaper Edition, for distribution, 2s. 6d.

Slade's (Rev. Canon) Twenty-one Prayers composed from
the Psalms for the Sick and Afflicted: with other Forms of Prayer, and
Hints and Directions for the Visitation of the Sick. Seventh Edition.
12mo. 3s. 6d.

Slade's (Rev. Canon) Plain Parochial Sermons. 7 vols. 12mo.
6s. each. Sold separately.

Smith's (Rev. J. G.) Life of Our Blessed Saviour: an
Epitome of the Gospel Narrative, arranged in order of time from the latest
Harmonies. With Introduction and Notes. Square 16mo. 2s.

Smith's (Rev. Dr. J. B.) Manual of the Rudiments of
Theology: containing an Abridgment of Tomline's Elements; an Analysis
of Paley's Evidences; a Summary of Pearson on the Creed; and a brief
Exposition of the Thirty-nine Articles, chiefly from Burnet; Explanation
of Jewish Rites and Ceremonies, &c. &c. Fifth Edition. 12mo. 8s. 6d.

Smith's (Rev. Dr. J. B.) Compendium of Rudiments in
Theology: containing a Digest of Bishop Butler's Analogy; an Epitome
of Dean Graves on the Pentateuch; and an Analysis of Bishop Newton
on the Prophecies. Second Edition. 12mo. 9s.

Stock's (Rev. John) Commentary on the First Epistle of
St. John. 8vo. 10s.

Talbot's (Hon. Mrs. J. C.) Parochial Mission-Women; their
Work and its Fruits. Second Edition. Small 8vo. In limp cloth, 2s.

Thornton's (Rev. T.) Life of Moses, in a Course of Village
Lectures; with a Preface Critical of Bishop Colenso's Work on the
Pentateuch. Small 8vo. 3s. 6d.

Threshold (The) of Private Devotion. Second Edition.
18mo. 2s.

Townsend's (Canon) Holy Bible, containing the Old and
New Testaments, arranged in Historical and Chronological Order. With
copious Notes and Indexes. Fifth Edition. In 2 vols., imperial 8vo.,
21s. each (sold separately).

Also, an Edition of this Arrangement of the Bible without the Notes,
in One Volume, 14s.

Trollope's (Rev. W.) Iliad of Homer from a carefully corrected Text; with copious English Notes, illustrating the Grammatical
Construction, the Manners and Customs, the Mythology and Antiquities
of the Heroic Ages; and Preliminary Observations on points of Classical
interest. Fifth Edition. 8vo. 15s.

Vidal's (Mrs.) Tales for the Bush. Originally published in Australia. Fourth Edition. Small 8vo. 5s.

Virgilii Æneidos Libri I—VI; with English Notes, chiefly from the Edition of P. Wagner, by T. Clayton, M.A., and C. S. Jerram, M.A. Small 8vo. 4s. 6d.

Warter's (Rev. J. W.) The Sea-board and the Down; or, My Parish in the South. In 2 vols. small 4to. Elegantly printed in Antique type, with Illustrations. 28s.

Webster's (Rev. W.) Syntax and Synonyms of the Greek Testament. 8vo. 9s.

The Syntax is based upon Donaldson's, with extracts from the writings of Archbishop Trench, Dean Alford, Dr. Wordsworth, but more especially from Bishop Ellicott, and the work on the Romans by Dr. Vaughan. Considerable use has also been made of the Article in the "Quarterly Review" for January, 1863.

The chapter on Synonyms treats of many words which have not been noticed by other writers. In another chapter attention is drawn to some passages in which the Authorized Version is incorrect, inexact, insufficient, or obscure. Copious Indices are added.

Welchman's Thirty-nine Articles of the Church of England, illustrated with Notes. New Edition. 2s. Or, interleaved with blank paper, 3s.

Wilberforce's (Bp. of Oxford) History of the Protestant Episcopal Church in America. Third Edition. Small 8vo. 5s.

Wilberforce's (Bp. of Oxford) Rocky Island, and other Similitudes. Twelfth Edition, with Cuts. 18mo. 2s. 6d.

Wilberforce's (Bp. of Oxford) Sermons preached before the Queen. Sixth Edition. 12mo. 6s.

Wilberforce's (Bp. of Oxford) Selection of Psalms and Hymns for Public Worship. New Edition. 32mo. 1s. each, or 3l. 10s. per hundred.

Williams's (Rev. Isaac) The Psalms interpreted of Christ; a Devotional Commentary. Vol. I. Small 8vo. 7s. 6d.

Williams's (Rev. Isaac) Devotional Commentary on the Gospel Narrative. 8 vols. small 8vo. 3l. 6s.

Sold separately as follows:—
Thoughts on the Study of the Gospels. 8s.
Harmony of the Evangelists. 8s. 6d.
The Nativity (extending to the Calling of St. Matthew). 8s. 6d.
Second Year of the Ministry. 8s.
Third Year of the Ministry. 8s. 6d.
The Holy Week. 8s. 6d.    The Passion. 8s.
The Resurrection. 8s.

Williams's (Rev. Isaac) Apocalypse, with Notes and Reflections. Small 8vo. 8s. 6d.

Williams's (Rev. Isaac) Beginning of the Book of Genesis, with Notes and Reflections. Small 8vo. 7s. 6d.

Williams's (Rev. Isaac) Sermons on the Characters of the Old Testament. Second Edition. 5s. 6d.

Williams's (Rev. Isaac) Female Characters of Holy Scripture; in a Series of Sermons. Second Edition. Small 8vo. 5s. 6d.

Williams's (Rev. Isaac) Plain Sermons on the Latter Part of the Catechism; being the Conclusion of the Series contained in the Ninth Volume of "Plain Sermons." 8vo. 6s. 6d.

Williams's (Rev. Isaac) Complete Series of Sermons on the Catechism. In one Volume. 13s.

Williams's (Rev. Isaac) Sermons on the Epistle and Gospel for the Sundays and Holy Days throughout the Year. Second Edition. In 3 vols. small 8vo. 16s. 6d.

\*\*\* The Third Volume, on the Saints' Days and other Holy Days of the Church, may be had separately, price 5s. 6d.

Williams's (Rev. Isaac) Christian Seasons; a Series of Poems. Small 8vo. 3s. 6d.

Willis (Rev. W. D.) on Simony. New Edition. 8vo. 7s. 6d.

Wilson's (Rev. Plumpton) Meditations and Prayers for Persons in Private. Fourth Edition, elegantly printed in 18mo. 4s. 6d.

Wilson's (late Bp. of Sodor and Man) Short and Plain Instruction for the Better Understanding of the Lord's Supper. To which is annexed, The Office of the Holy Communion, with Proper Helps and Directions. Pocket size, 1s. Also, a larger Edition, 2s.

Wilson's (late Bp. of Sodor and Man) Sacra Privata; Private Meditations and Prayers. Pocket size, 1s. Also, a larger Edition, 2s.

These two Works may be had in various bindings.

Woodward's (Rev. F. B.) Tracts and Sermons on Subjects of the Day; with an Appendix on the Roman Catholic Controversy. 12mo. 7s.

Wordsworth's (late Rev. Dr.) Ecclesiastical Biography; or, Lives of Eminent Men connected with the History of Religion in England, from the Commencement of the Reformation to the Revolution. Selected, and Illustrated with Notes. Fourth Edition. In 4 vols. 8vo. With 5 Portraits. 2l. 14s.

Wordsworth's (Bp. of St. Andrew's) Christian Boyhood at a Public School; a Collection of Sermons and Lectures delivered at Winchester College from 1836 to 1846. In 2 vols. 8vo. 1l. 4s.

Wordsworth's (Bp. of St. Andrew's) Catechesis; or, Christian Instruction preparatory to Confirmation and First Communion. Third Edition. Crown 8vo. 3s. 6d.

Wordsworth's (Archd.) New Testament of our Lord and Saviour Jesus Christ, in the original Greek. With Notes, Introductions, and Indexes. New Edition. In Two Vols., imperial 8vo. 4l.

*Separately,*

Part I.: The Four Gospels. 1l. 1s.
Part II.: The Acts of the Apostles. 10s. 6d.
Part III.: The Epistles of St. Paul. 1l. 11s. 6d.
Part IV.: The General Epistles and Book of Revelation; with Indexes. 1l. 1s.

Wordsworth's (Archd.) The Holy Bible. With Notes and Introductions. Part I., containing Genesis and Exodus. Imperial 8vo. 21s. Part II., Leviticus to Deuteronomy. 18s.

Wordsworth's (Archd.) Occasional Sermons preached in Westminster Abbey. In 7 vols. 8vo. Vols. I., II., and III., 7s. each— Vols. IV. and V., 8s. each—Vol. VI., 7s.—Vol. VII., 6s.

Wordsworth's (Archd.) Theophilus Anglicanus; or, Instruction concerning the Principles of the Church Universal and the Church of England. Ninth Edition. Small 8vo. 5s.

Wordsworth's (Archd.) Elements of Instruction on the Church; being an Abridgment of the above. Second Edition. 2s.

Wordsworth's (Archd.) Journal of a Tour in Italy; with Reflections on the Present Condition and Prospects of Religion in that Country. Second Edition. 2 vols. post 8vo. 15s.

Wordsworth's (Archd.) On the Interpretation of the Bible. Five Lectures delivered at Westminster Abbey. 3s. 6d.

Wordsworth's (Archd.) Holy Year: Hymns for Sundays and Holydays, and for other Occasions; with a preface on Hymnology. Third Edition, in larger type, square 16mo., cloth extra, 4s. 6d. Also an Edition with Tunes, 4s. 6d.; and a cheap Edition, 6d.

Worgan's (Rev. J. H.) Divine Week; or, Outlines of a Harmony of the Geologic Periods with the Mosaic "Days" of Creation. Crown 8vo. 5s.

Yonge's (C. D.) History of England from the Earliest Times to the Peace of Paris, 1856. With a Chronological Table of Contents. In one thick volume, crown 8vo. 12s.

Though available as a School-book, this volume contains as much as three ordinary octavos. It is written on a carefully digested plan, ample space being given to the last three centuries. All the best authorities have been consulted.

A

# SELECTION FROM THE SCHOOL SERIES

OF THE

## REV. THOMAS KERCHEVER ARNOLD, M.A.

LATE FELLOW OF TRINITY COLLEGE, CAMBRIDGE.

**Practical Introductions to Greek, Latin, &c.**

Henry's First Latin Book. Eighteenth Edition. 12mo. 3s.

The object of this work is to enable the youngest boys to master the principal difficulties of the Latin language by easy steps, and to furnish older students with a Manual for Self-Tuition.

Great attention has lately been given to the improvement of what may be called its mechanical parts. The Vocabularies have been much extended, and greater uniformity of reference has been secured. A few rules have been omitted or simplified. Every thing has been done which the long experience of the Editor, or the practice of his friends in their own schools has shown to be desirable.

At the same time, no pains have been spared to do this without altering in any way the character of the work, or making it inconvenient to use it side by side with copies of earlier editions.

Supplementary Exercises to Henry's First Latin Book. By G. D. Hill, B.A. 2s.

A Second Latin Book, and Practical Grammar. Intended as a Sequel to Henry's First Latin Book. Eighth Edition. 12mo. 4s.

A First Verse Book, Part I.; intended as an easy Introduction to the Latin Hexameter and Pentameter. Eighth Edition. 12mo. 2s. Part II.; Additional Exercises. 1s.

Historiæ Antiquæ Epitome, from *Cornelius Nepos, Justin*, &c. With English Notes, Rules for Construing, Questions, Geographical Lists, &c. Seventh Edition. 4s.

A First Classical Atlas, containing fifteen Maps, coloured in outline; intended as a Companion to the *Historiæ Antiquæ Epitome*. 8vo. 7s. 6d.

A Practical Introduction to Latin Prose Composition. Part I. Thirteenth Edition. 8vo. 6s. 6d.

This Work is founded on the principles of imitation and frequent repetition. It is at once a Syntax, a Vocabulary, and an Exercise Book; and considerable attention has been paid to the subject of Synonymes. It is now used at all, or nearly all, the public schools.

A Practical Introduction to Latin Prose Composition, Part II.; containing the Doctrine of Latin Particles, with Vocabulary, an Antibarbarus, &c. Fourth Edition. 8vo. 8s.

A Practical Introduction to Latin Verse Composition. Fourth and Cheaper Edition, considerably revised. 12mo. 3s. 6d.

This Work supposes the pupil to be already capable of composing verses easily when the "*full sense*" is given. Its object is to facilitate his transition to original composition in Elegiacs and Hexameters, and to teach him to compose the Alcaic and Sapphic stanzas: explanations and a few exercises are also given on the other Horatian metres. A short Poetical Phraseology is added.

In the present Edition the whole work has been corrected, the translations being carefully compared with the originals. The Alcaics and Sapphics have been arranged in stanzas, and each kind of verse placed in a separate chapter, the old numbers of the Exercises being preserved for convenience in use. Other improvements have been made which it is hoped will add to its value.

Gradus ad Parnassum Novus Anticlepticus; founded on Quicherat's *Thesaurus Poeticus Linguæ Latinæ*. 8vo. *half-bound*. 10s. 6d.

\*\*\* A Prospectus, with specimen page, may be had of the Publishers.

Longer Latin Exercises, Part I. Third Edition. 8vo. 4s.

The object of this Work is to supply boys with an easy collection of *short* passages, as an Exercise Book for those who have gone once, at least, through the First Part of the Editor's "Practical Introduction to Latin Prose Composition."

Longer Latin Exercises, Part II.; containing a Selection of Passages of greater length, in genuine idiomatic English, for Translation into Latin. 8vo. 4s.

Materials for Translation into Latin: selected and arranged by Augustus Grotefend. Translated from the German by the Rev. H. H. Arnold, B.A., with Notes and Excursuses. Third Edition. 8vo. 7s. 6d.

A Copious and Critical English-Latin Lexicon, by the Rev. T. K. Arnold and the Rev. J. E. Riddle. Sixth Edition. 1l. 5s.

An Abridgment of the above Work, for the Use of Schools. By the Rev. J. C. Ebden, late Fellow and Tutor of Trinity Hall, Cambridge. Square 12mo. *bound*. 10s. 6d.

---

The First Greek Book; on the Plan of "Henry's First Latin Book." Fifth Edition. 12mo. 5s.

The Second Greek Book (on the same Plan); containing an Elementary Treatise on the Greek Particles and the Formation of Greek Derivatives. 12mo. 5s. 6d.

A Practical Introduction to Greek Accidence. With Easy Exercises and Vocabulary. Seventh Edition. 8vo. 5s. 6d.

A Practical Introduction to Greek Prose Composition, Part I. Tenth Edition. 8vo. 5s. 6d.

>   The object of this Work is to enable the Student, as soon as he can decline and conjugate with tolerable facility, to translate simple sentences after given examples, and with given words; the principles trusted to being principally those of *imitation and very frequent repetition.* It is at once a Syntax, a Vocabulary, and an Exercise Book.

Professor Madvig's Syntax of the Greek Language, especially of the Attic Dialect; translated by the Rev. Henry Browne, M.A. Together with an Appendix on the Greek Particles; by the Translator. Square 8vo. 8s. 6d.

An Elementary Greek Grammar. 12mo. 5s.; or, with Dialects, 6s.

A Complete Greek and English Lexicon for the Poems of Homer, and the Homeridæ. Translated from the German of Crusius, by Professor Smith. New and Revised Edition. 9s. *half-bound.*

\*\*\* A Prospectus and specimen of this Lexicon may be had.

A Copious Phraseological English-Greek Lexicon, founded on a work prepared by J. W. Frädersdorff, Ph. Dr. of the Taylor-Institution, Oxford. Revised, Enlarged, and Improved by the Rev. T. K. Arnold, M.A., formerly Fellow of Trinity College, Cambridge, and Henry Browne, M.A., Vicar of Pevensey, and Prebendary of Chichester. Third Edition, corrected, with the Appendix incorporated. 8vo. 21s.

\*\*\* A Prospectus, with specimen page, may be had.

---

Classical Examination Papers. A Series of 93 Extracts from Greek, Roman, and English Classics for Translation, with occasional Questions and Notes; each extract on a separate leaf. Price of the whole in a specimen packet, 4s., or six copies of any Separate Paper may be had for 3d.

---

Keys to the following may be had by Tutors only:

First Latin Book, 1s.        Second Latin Book, 2s.
        Cornelius Nepos, 1s.
First Verse Book, 1s.        Latin Verse Composition, 2s.
   Latin Prose Composition, Parts I. and II., 1s. 6d. each.
Longer Latin Exercises, Part I., 1s. 6d.        Part II., 2s. 6d.
   Greek Prose Composition, Part I., 1s. 6d.    Part II., 4s. 6d.
        First Greek Book, 1s. 6d.    Second, 2s.

ARNOLD'S SCHOOL SERIES. 21

The First Hebrew Book; on the Plan of "Henry's First Latin Book." 12mo. Second Edition. 7s. 6d. The Key. Second Edition. 3s. 6d.

The Second Hebrew Book, containing the Book of Genesis; together with a Hebrew Syntax, and a Vocabulary and Grammatical Commentary. 9s.

---

The First German Book; on the Plan of "Henry's First Latin Book." By the Rev. T. K. Arnold and Dr. Frädersdorff. Fifth Edition. 12mo. 5s. 6d. The Key, 2s. 6d.

A Reading Companion to the First German Book; containing Extracts from the best Authors with a Vocabulary and Notes. 12mo. Second Edition. 4s.

---

The First French Book; on the Plan of "Henry's First Latin Book." Fifth Edition. 12mo. 5s. 6d. Key to the Exercises, by Delille, 2s. 6d.

---

Henry's English Grammar; a Manual for Beginners. 12mo. 3s. 6d.

Spelling turned Etymology. Second Edition. 12mo. 2s. 6d.

The Pupil's Book, (a Companion to the above,) 1s. 3d.

Latin viâ English; being the Second Part of the above Work. Second Edition. 12mo. 4s. 6d.

An English Grammar for Classical Schools; being a Practical Introduction to "English Prose Composition." Sixth Edition. 12mo. 4s. 6d.

---

## Handbooks for the Classical Student, with Questions.

Ancient History and Geography. Translated from the German of Pütz, by the Ven. Archdeacon Paul. Second Edition. 12mo. 6s. 6d.

Mediæval History and Geography. Translated from the German of Pütz. By the same. 12mo. 4s. 6d.

Modern History and Geography. Translated from the German of Pütz. By the same. 12mo. 5s. 6d.

Grecian Antiquities. By Professor Bojesen. Translated from the German Version of Dr. Hoffa. By the same. Second Edition. 12mo. 3s. 6d.

Roman Antiquities. By Professor Bojesen. Second Edition. 3s. 6d.

Hebrew Antiquities. By the Rev. Henry Browne, M.A. Prebendary of Chichester. 12mo. 4s.

*⁎* This Work describes the manners and customs of the ancient Hebrews which were common to them with other nations, and the rites and ordinances which distinguished them as the chosen people Israel.

Greek Synonymes. From the French of Pillon. 6s. 6d.

Latin Synonymes. From the German of Döderlein. Translated by the Rev. H. H. Arnold. Second Edition. 4s.

## Arnold's School Classics.

Cornelius Nepos, Part I.; with Critical Questions and Answers, and an imitative Exercise on each Chapter. Fourth Edition. 12mo. 4s.

Eclogæ Ovidianæ, with English Notes; Part I. (from the Elegiac Poems.) Tenth Edition. 12mo. 2s. 6d.

Eclogæ Ovidianæ, Part II. (from the Metamorphoses.) 5s.

The Æneid of Virgil, with English Notes. 12mo. 6s.

The Works of Horace, followed by English Introductions and Notes, adapted for School use. 12mo. 7s.

Cicero.—Selections from his Orations, with English Notes, from the best and most recent sources. Contents:—The Fourth Book of the Impeachment of Verres, the Four Speeches against Catiline, and the Speech for the Poet Archias. Second Edition. 12mo. 4s.

Cicero, Part II.; containing Selections from his Epistles, arranged in the order of time, with Accounts of the Consuls, Events of each year, &c. With English Notes from the best Commentators, especially Matthiæ. 12mo. 5s.

Cicero, Part III.; containing the Tusculan Disputations (entire). With English Notes from Tischer, by the Rev. Archdeacon Paul. Second Edition. 5s. 6d.

Cicero, Part IV.; containing De Finibus Malorum et Bonorum. (On the Supreme Good.) With a Preface, English Notes, &c., partly from Madvig and others, by the Rev James Beaven, D.D., late Professor of Theology in King's College, Toronto. 12mo. 5s. 6d.

Cicero, Part V. ; containing Cato Major, sive De Senectute
Dialogus; with English Notes from Sommerbrodt, by the Rev. Henry
Browne, M.A., Canon of Chichester. 12mo. 2s. 6d.

Homer for Beginners.—The First Three Books of the Iliad,
with English Notes; forming a sufficient Commentary for Young Students.
Third Edition. 12mo. 3s. 6d.

Homer.—The Iliad Complete, with English Notes and
Grammatical References. Third Edition. In one thick volume, 12mo.
half-bound 12s.

In this Edition, the Argument of each Book is divided into short Sections, which are prefixed to those portions of the Text, respectively, which they describe. The Notes (principally from Dübner) are at the foot of each page. At the end of the volume are useful Appendices.

Homer.—The Iliad, Books I. to IV. ; with a Critical Introduction, and copious English Notes. Second Edition. 12mo. 7s. 6d.

Demosthenes, with English Notes from the best and most
recent sources, Sauppe, Doberenz. Jacobs, Dissen, Westermann, &c.
The Olynthiac Orations. Second Edition. 12mo. 3s.
The Oration on the Crown. Second Edition. 12mo. 4s. 6d.
The Philippic Orations. Second Edition. 12mo. 4s.

Æschines.—Speech against Ctesiphon. 12mo. 4s.

The Text is that of *Baiter* and *Sauppe;* the Notes are by Professor Champlin, with additional Notes by President Woolsey and the Editor.

Sophocles, with English Notes, from Schneidewin. By the
Ven. Archdeacon Paul, and the Rev. Henry Browne, M.A.
The Ajax. 3s.—The Philoctetes. 3s.—The Œdipus Tyrannus. 4s.—
The Œdipus Coloneus. 4s.—The Antigone. 4s.

Euripides, with English Notes, from Hartung, Dübner,
Witzschel, Schöne, &c.
The Hecuba.—The Hippolytus.—The Bacchæ.—The Medea.—The
Iphigenia in Tauris, 3s. *each.*

Aristophanes.—Eclogæ Aristophanicæ, with English Notes,
by Professor Felton. Part I. (The Clouds.) 12mo. 3s. 6d. Part II.
(The Birds.) 3s. 6d.

\*\*\* *In this Edition the objectionable passages are omitted.*

---

**A Descriptive Catalogue of the whole of Arnold's School Series, may be had gratis.**
**Also, Rivington's complete Classified School Catalogue.**

*Publishing Monthly, price 1s.*

# The Englishman's Magazine

OF

LITERATURE, RELIGION, SCIENCE, AND ART.

---

Contents of No. 10, for October, 1865.

1. THE SEA-SIDE. *By George Tugwell, M.A., Author of "A Manual of the Sea Anemones."* II. Down among the Tangles.
2. HARVEST HOME.
3. STRAY THOUGHTS ON FAILURES.
4. SOME ACCOUNT OF BARRACK-LIFE IN INDIA. *By an Officer there.*
5. CANTERBURY AND THE PRIMATES.
6. THE ORPHAN CHORISTER.
7. THE OLD PAGODA TREE. A Story in Five Parts. *By Iltudus T. Prichard, Author of "How to Manage it," "Mutinies in Rajpootana," &c.*
    Part III.   Chapter VII.—A Friend in Need.
    Chapter VIII.—The Temple-cave.
    Chapter IX.—Captivity.
8. THE POWER OF THOUGHT. *Imitated from Calderon. By Archdeacon Churton.*
9. MAN BEFORE HISTORY. *By T. G. Bonney, M.A., F.G.S.* II. The Lakes, Shores, and Morasses.
10. "WE ARE."
11. ST. CHARLES BORROMEO.
12. RENDERINGS FROM THE GERMAN.—Song of Liberty.—The Night Ride.

---

### RIVINGTONS,
LONDON, OXFORD, AND CAMBRIDGE.

www.ingramcontent.com/pod-product-compliance
Lightning Source LLC
Chambersburg PA
CBHW031951230426
43672CB00010B/2121